製作／笹原 大

HOW TO BUILD 1/700 現用航空母艦 ハンドブック

HOW TO BUILD 1/700 SCALE MODERN AIRCRAFT CARRIER HANDBOOK

DAINIPPONKAIGA

Dai Sasahara 笹原 大

1969年生。千葉県出身。中学生までガンプラをメインに楽しんでいたが、高校入学と共に製作活動を休止する。サラリーマンを約20年経験後、転勤のない現在の仕事に就いたため、家族の了解もあり模型製作を再開。現在、『ネイビーヤード』誌をメインに1/700スケールの日本海軍艦艇製作に特化した模型ライフを楽しんでいる。二児の父親。ブログ名R＆R工廠の由来は子供の名前のイニシャルから命名

Born in Chiba Prefecture in 1969. Until junior high school, He use to build a Gundam model mainly. He stopped producing after entering high school. After about 20 years of office working, he settled with current job which doesn't have to transfer. Therefore, with the consent of the family, he resumed making the model. Currently, he specializes in the production of 1/700 scale Japanese naval vessels on the Navy Yard magazine, enjoying his modeler life. The father of two children. Blog Name The R&R factory is named after the child's initials.

PIT-ROAD 1/700 Scale USS Nimitz (CVN-68)

米国海軍 原子力空母 CVN-68 ニミッツ
ピットロード 1/700 インジェクションプラスチックキット

PIT-ROAD 1/700 USS Nimitz (CVN-68)
Injection plastic kit

艦載機のための台座たる空母に乗った、極小の"飛行機模型"

このページで紹介する空母ニミッツは、もともとは航空機模型専門誌『スケールアヴィエーション』のコンベンション用に製作した1/700のF-14トムキャットの展示ベースとして製作がスタートしたもの。しかし笹原氏の作る空母、ただの展示ベースで終わるわけがない。細部まで精密に作り込むというこれまでの作品に加えて、あらたに電飾を組み込み格納庫や艦橋を光らせることにもチャンレジしている。貪欲に新技法を取り入れる氏の真骨頂を本作に見た

The aircraft carrier Nimitz, which is introduced on this page, was originally built as an exhibition base for the 1/700 F -14 Tomcat, which was produced for the convention on Scale Aviation magazine. But Sasahara's aircraft carrier cannot end up being just an exhibition. Just like his previous work, which was detailed and modded, he added lighting system to it's hangars and bridge. This work shows the true essence of Sasahara who eagerly incorporates new techniques to his new work

現代における世界最大、最強の軍艦

ニミッツ級原子力空母は1970年代から現在まで、40年以上にわたって整備された世界最大の軍艦だ。その同型艦は10隻に及ぶ。新造時の搭載機は80〜105機を予定していたが、その後、搭載機の大型化なども進み、現在では56機プラスヘリコプター15機の71機程度で運用されている。
作例の「ニミッツ」は1980年ごろの状態を再現したもので搭載機は艦上戦闘機F-14トムキャット、艦上攻撃機A-6イントルーダー、艦上攻撃機A-4コルセア、電子戦機EA-6プラウラー、早期警戒機E-2Cホークアイなど。現在ではこれらの機体はほとんど退役し艦上戦闘機、艦上攻撃機はすべてFA-18ホーネット／スーパーホ-ネット系列のものへと置き換えられている

The Nimitz-class nuclear-powered aircraft carrier is the world's largest warship that has been in service for more than 40 years since the 1970s. There are as many as 10 such ships. When the ship was newly built, it was planned to carry 80 to 105 aircraft, but the size of the aircraft has increased since then, and currently it carries about 71 aircraft, including 15 helicopters. This Sasahara's "Nimitz" is simulating her state in 1980s and on board the carrier are F -14 Tomcat, A-6 Intruder, A-4 Corsair, the electronic warfare aircraft EA-6 Prowler, and Early-warning aircraft E-2C Hawkeye, etc. At present, most of these aircrafts have been retired, and carrier-based fighters and carrier-based attack aircraft have all been replaced by FA-18 Hornet/Super Hornet.

空母機動部隊の主役と言えば、いうまでもなく艦載機であろう(断言)。そもそもが航空母艦は艦載機を飛ばして色々な任務をやらせるための船であり、そのためにあれだけ巨大な船体と設備が必要なのだ。

そのような艦載機と航空母艦のプライオリティーの順番で言うと、今回笹原氏が製作したのは1/700スケールのF-14であり、ニミッツはそのF-14のための巨大な土台である、ということになる。これはただの言葉遊びではない。「1/700サイズでどこまで精密にトムキャットを作ることができるか挑戦したい」というものであり、まず余人には到達できないほど小さくて緻密なF-14を作る、というのが目的だったのである。

だからこの作品のF-14には、通常の艦船模型のセオリーから外れるほどの手間と熱量がつぎ込まれている。なんせ使っている排気ノズルの部品はアドラーズネストによる特注品。キャノピーもヒートプレスによる自作。シートや兵装は作り直し、よく見ると赤いフライトタグすらついているという、1/700スケールの「飛行機模型」と言い切って遜色のない作り込みが行なわれているのだ。そしてその主役を引き立たせるための土台として、フルハルの航空母艦という素材は申し分のないものなのである。飛行機模型専門誌である『スケールアヴィエーション』にいきなり航空母艦が掲載された理由。それはこの笹原氏による極小のF-14の群れが、紛れもなく最高の出来映えの飛行機模型だからなのだ。 ■

Needless to say, carrier-based aircraft play a major role in the aircraft carrier task force. In the first place, an aircraft carrier is a ship that can launch carrier-based aircraft to perform various duties, and therefore needs such a huge hull and equipment. With that order in mined, Sasahara built the 1/700 scale F -14 first and Nimitz is a huge base for those F-14s. This is not just a word game. The idea was to "How precisely I can make a Tomcat with 1/700 size." and to make the F -14 so small and precise that other people could not recreate it.

That's why the F -14 received so much more attention than the traditional ship modeling works. The parts of the exhaust nozzle used are custom made by Adler's Nest. The canopy is handmade by heat press. The seats and weapons are redesigned, and even have a red flight tag, making it a detailed 1/700 scale "airplane model." And the Fll Hull aircraft carrier is perfect material as a basis for the highlight of its star. The reason why the aircraft carrier was published in this magazine, which specializes in airplane models. That's because Sasahara's tiny fleet of F-14s are undoubtedly the great model of planes.

本作品の主役であるF-14トムキャットは駐機状態のものと発艦準備状態の2種類製作。駐機仕様は主翼を後退状態とし、水平尾翼を後ろに下げてキャノピーを上げている仕様に。発艦準備仕様はその逆で、主翼を展開させてフラップを下げる、水平尾翼は水平、もしくは前方を下げて発艦時の状態にしている。エンジンノズルはアドラーズネストに依頼して特別に製作してもらった真ちゅう挽物。このノズルのおかげで引き締まった機体が再現できた、とのこと

The F-14 Tomcat, the main character of this work, is made in 2 kinds, one is in the parking state and the other is in the ready state. In the parking state, the main wings are swept rearward, horizontal stabilizers are lowered and the canopy is in raised position. The specifications for the launching positions aircrafts are the opposite. The main wings are fowared position, the flaps are lowered, and the horizontal stabilizers are in launching position. The engine nozzles are made specially by Adler's Nest. Thanks to the nozzle, the fighter looks very sharp for its size.

製作にあたってはキットの他にファイブスターモデルとビッグブルーボーイなどから販売されているニミッツ級用エッチングパーツを多数用意し、その中から出来の良い物を適宜組み合わせてディテールアップをはかった。特に艦橋の上に配置されているマストやその周辺のレーダー類は全てエッチングパーツの集合体となっているのだが、このあたりのディテールは正直不明な点も多かったため、要素の取捨選択は「勘」による、というのが製作した笹原氏の弁である。また甲板上に取り付けられているカタパルトもすべてエッチングパーツによる再現だ。

これらのエッチングパーツは船体だけではなく艦載機のディテールアップにも役立てられている。例えばF-14の着陸脚などは前述のビッグブルーボーイ製エッチングパーツを使っており、より緻密な印象となっている。他に機体のディテールアップに使ったパーツとしては、アドラーズネストがこの作品のために特注で製作した排気ノズルの金属製パーツがある。これらを使用することで、多数の艦載機がピリッとした印象に仕上がった

In addition to the kit, Nimitz-class etching parts by FiveStar Model and Big Blue Boy were prepared, and the details were improved by combining those good quality parts. In particular, all the masts placed on the bridge and radars around it are an assembly of etched parts, but there are many unclear points about the details in this area, so Sasahara's used his intuition detailing those areas. All the catapults on the deck are also etched.

These etching parts are used not only to improve the hull but also to improve the details of the carrier-based aircraft. For example, the F-14 landing gear uses the Big Blue Boy photo etching parts, giving it a more detailed look. Other parts used to add detail of the fuselage include a metal exhaust nozzle specially made by Adler's Nest. By using them, those aircraft's detail became more precise.

艦橋付近に配置しているホークアイとプラウラーは各機体の写真集を参考にフラップ等も自作して再現。また、アクセントとしてフォークリフト・クレーン車はビッグブルーボーイ製のエッチングパーツを使用してワイヤーなどを追加工作して仕上げている。艦橋のレーダー類はもう少し調べてじっくり作りこみたかったが資料が少なくて断念した箇所

The Hawkeye and Prowler, which are located near the bridge, have been recreated with moddified flaps and other items based on real photographs of each aircraft. As an accent, the forklift and crane truck is finished with additional work such as wires using photo etching parts by Big Blue Boy. The radars of the bridge needed little bit more research butr with very few documents and references he had to give up for more detail.

PIT-ROAD 1/700 Scale USS Nimitz (CVN-68)

How To Build PIT-ROAD 1/700 Scale USS Nimitz (CVN-68)

1

船体下部を裏返し全体にヤスリ掛けをしてヒケなどのチェックを行なう。中央付近のふたつの穴は台座固定用ナットを埋め込むためのもの

The bottom part of the hull is sanded to check for sink marks. The two holes in the center are used to insert a mounting nut.

2

各部の加工を始める前に、展示用の台座に飾り支柱を立てて船体を仮固定し確認を行なう。台座はすべてオーダーメイドで外注している

Before the processing of each part, the hull is temporarily fixed and confirmed by putting an ornamental post on the display pedestal. All pedestals are custom-made.

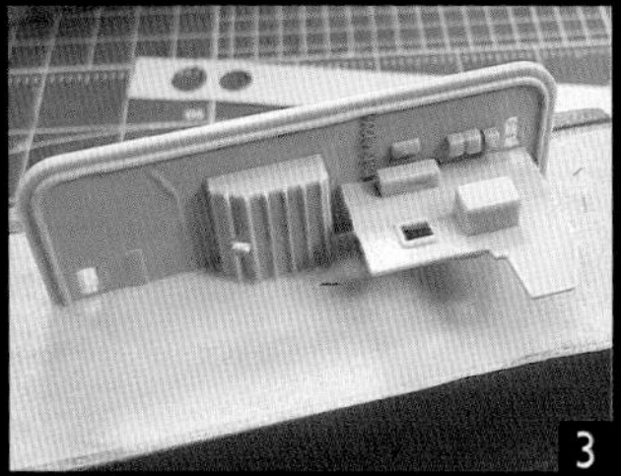

3

艦尾隔壁部。奥まった位置に固定されるパーツなので船体に納める前に作り込みを行なう。手摺や、中央付近にモンキーラッタルを追加した

The bulkhead of the stern. Since it is a part will be fixed inside, it is worked on before put into the hull. We added handrails and monkey lattals near the center.

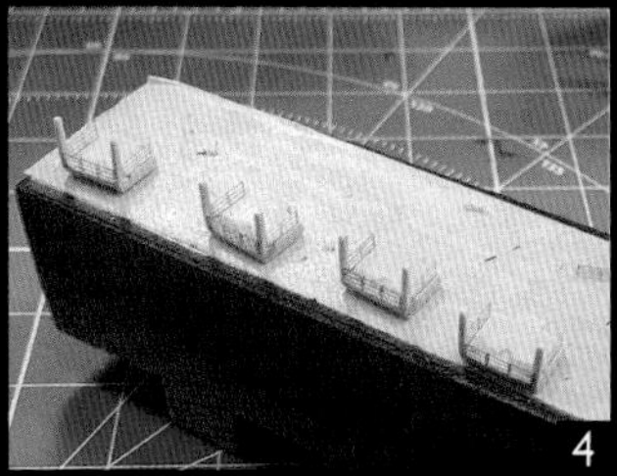

4

格納庫内の4カ所あるバルコニーのパーツにも手摺をつける。取り付けた手摺に歪みがないか、垂直は出ているかを入念にチェックする

Four balcony parts in the hangar fixed with handrails. Carefully check whether the attached handrailis not distorted.

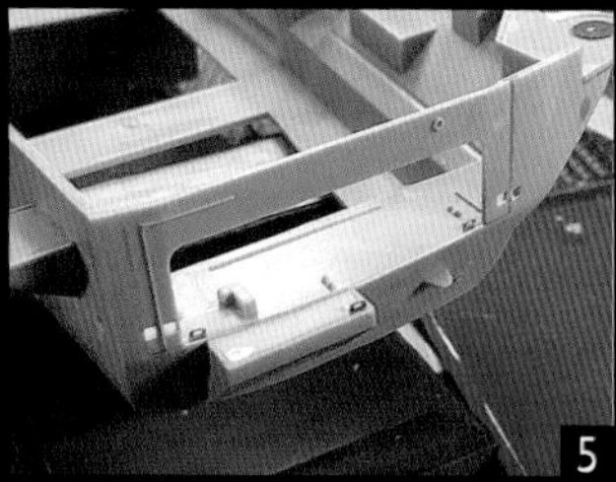

5

緑色の部分はパテ。パーツ同士の嵌合の悪さゆえ、かなり隙間ができる。3つのフェアリーダーはエッチングパーツでディテールアップ

The green part is putty. Due to the poor fitting between the parts, there is a considerable gap. The three fairleads are detailed with photo etched parts.

6

エッチング製のミサイルランチャー。歪みなく直角に折り曲げられているが、ご覧通りそのサイズは長辺で5mmほど。丁寧な作業のたまもの

An photo etched parts missile launcher. It is bent at right angles without distortion, but as you can see, it is about 5mm long. Result of careful work.

7

ミサイルランチャーに支柱をつけて船体に仮置き。小さいパーツだが、実際に置いて設置場所やサイズの違和感がないか、を必ず確認する

A prop was attached to the missile launcher and placed temporarily on the hull. Although it is a small part, make sure that there is no conflict in the installation place.

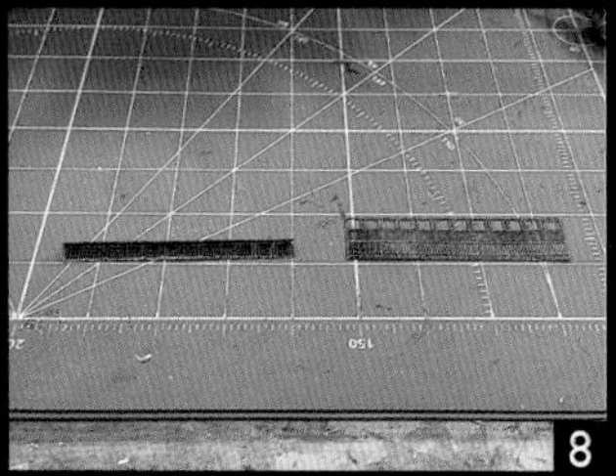

8

エレベーターに取り付ける落下防止用ネット。右は加工前の状態。単に折り曲げるのではなく、適度なたわみなども表現するのがポイント

Fall prevention net installed in the elevator. Right is before machining. It is important to express the moderate deflection instead of simply bending it.

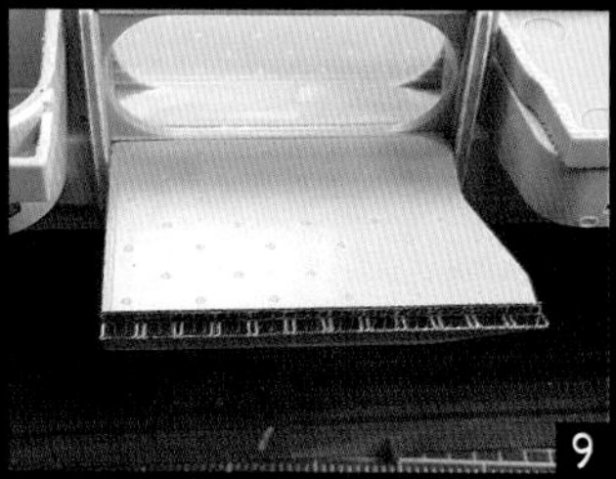

9

エレベーターに取り付けた状態。一見、単純なパーツに見えるが完成後もアイキャッチとなる部分でもあり、水平・垂直はきっちりチェック

Installed in the elevator. It is a simple part, but it is also a part that can be used as an eye catch after completion. All angles are checked thoroughly.

10

エレベーターに艦載機を載せる。水平・垂直やバランスの確認をしつつ、完成状態をイメージすることでモチベーションアップにもつながる

Place an aircraft on the elevator. The image of the completed state while checking the horizontal, vertical and balance.

11

艦橋の曲面ガラスは電飾を仕込むため透明プラ板を写真右手にある丸棒に巻きつけ、お湯をかけて形状出しを行ないクリアグリーンで塗装

The curved glass of the Bridge is shaped by wrapping a transparent plastic plate around the round bar and pouring hot water on it. Painted with clear green.

12

窓下方の外周部はプラ材を巻いて加工、段差などのディテールも再現。窓枠にはエッチングパーツを使用。ここでも水平には気をつける

The outer frame of the lower part of the window is made of plastic and details such as steps are reproduced. Etched part is used for the window frame.

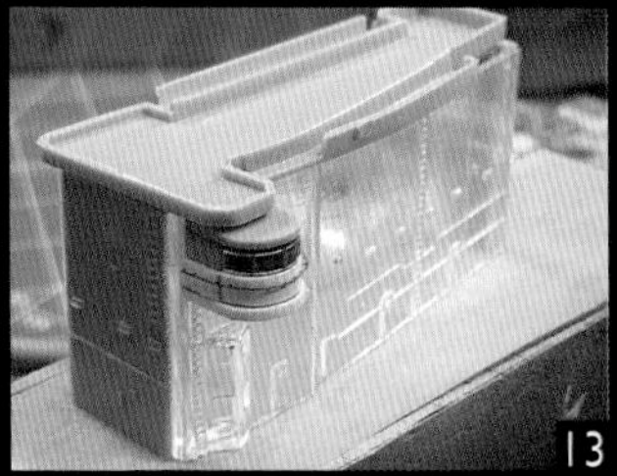

13

完成したパーツを艦橋に取り付け確認。この確認作業が幾度となく行なわれる理由は、実際に組み上げた状態での違和感を感じ取るため

The completed parts were installed on the bridge. Repeat temporary assembles to see if there are any mismatched in size or placement.

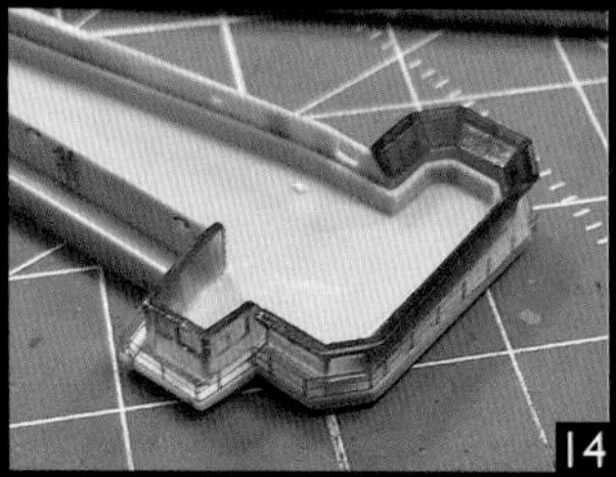

14

この窓ガラスはキットのパーツそのまま。クリア成型されているので組んでからマスキングし、クリアグリーンを吹き付け塗装している

This window part is from the kit. Since it is clear molded, it is masked after assembling, and clear green is sprayed and painted.

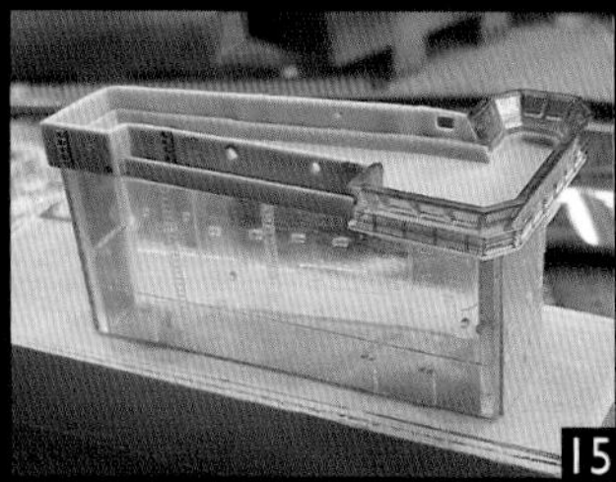

15

艦橋にフロアパーツを乗せた状態。資料を見ながら、ここで梯子などのディテールを汎用エッチングパーツなどを用いて追加していく

Floor parts are on the bridge. Using refference material for adding more details such as ladder with general photo etched parts.

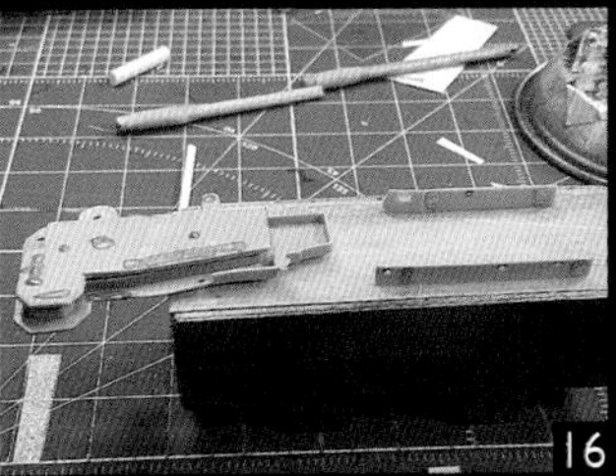

16

天井部分のパーツを取り付ける。キットパーツを取り付けるための穴などは一旦パテで塞ぐ。また電飾を施すため隙間ができないか、も確認

Install ceiling parts. The holes for parts fitting should be covered with putty. Also, check if there are no gaps due to the electric decoration.

17

ここでエッチングパーツも取り付ける。LEDを点灯させて光漏れがないかチェック。隙間ができるようであれば延ばしランナーで埋めていく

The photo etched part is also attached here. Turn on the LED and check for light leakage. If there is a gap, fill it with the stretched plastic rod.

18

艦橋トップ部分のマスト。ここは専用エッチングパーツを使用している。取り付けには歪みや傾きがないか、細心の注意を払う

The mast at the top of a ship's bridge. Dedicated photo etched parts are used. Pay close attention to any distortion or tilt when you install it.

19

艦橋トップのアンテナ類。手摺やアンテナは真ちゅう線や汎用エッチングパーツを加工し、写真資料を見ながらバランスを調整していく

The antennas at the top of the bridge. Brass wires and photo etching parts are used for the handrails, antennas, and the balance is adjusted according to reference materials.

20

レーダー類はキット付属のエッチングパーツを使用。ドーム型のものはキットにパーツが用意されるが野暮ったく感じるため自作した

For the radars, use the etching parts provided with the kit. The dome-shaped ones are scratch built for better quality.

21

各種アンテナをベース部分に固定したところ。組み上がりの水平・垂直を愚直に確認し、問題が無ければこのまま塗装に入る準備となる

The various antennas are fixed to the base. Check the angles and if there is no problem, we will prepare for painting.

22

最終的な組み上がりのチェック。360°全方向から舐めるように見て、歪みが無いことを確認。とにかくあらゆる角度から見ることが大切

Check the final composition. Check that there is no distortion by inspect it from all 360 degrees. it's important to look at the model from every angle.

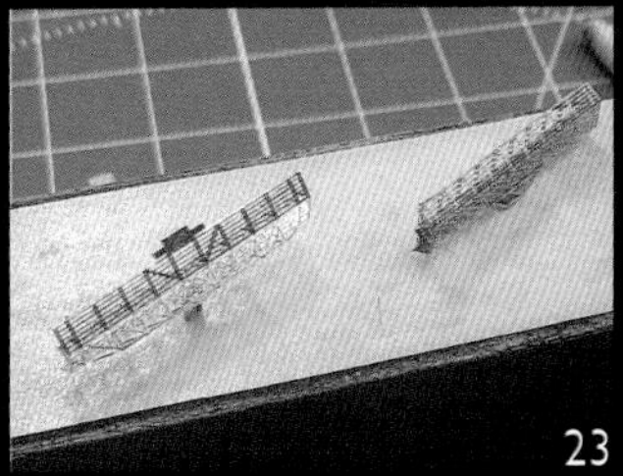

23

大型レーダーはエッチングパーツを使用。写真の左右は異なるメーカーの製品。実際に組んでみて見栄えの良かった左側の製品を使用した

Photo etched parts is used for large radar. Tried few options and one on the lest one was used because of better looks.

24

組み上げたエッチングパーツを載せた艦橋後方のレーダーヤード。形状の正確さだけでなく立体物としてのサイズ感やバランスも重要視する

Radar yard behind the Bridge. Emphasis is placed not only on the accuracy of the shape but also on the sense of size and balance as a three-dimensional object.

25

艦橋にもアンテナやレーダーといった艤装も進めていく。電飾を点灯させ雰囲気を確認しつつ、光漏れなどがないかも再度、確認していく

The ship's bridge will also be outfitted with antennas and radar. Turn on the lights to check the atmosphere, and check again if there is any light leakage.

26

さらにアンテナや手摺などを取り付け、ほぼ完成状態の艦橋。手前にある1円玉からその驚異的なサイズと精度を推し量ることができる

The bridge is almost complete with antennas and handrails. You can guess its amazing size and accuracy from the coin in front.

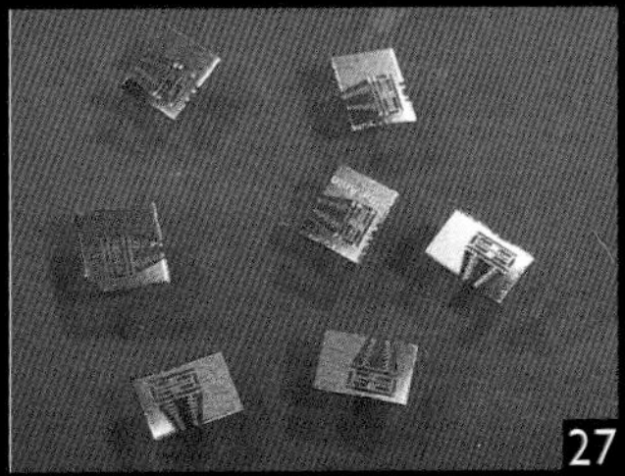

27

艦橋の周囲に取り付けられた虫のような形をしたアンテナは、このエッチングパーツを折り曲げ加工し組み立てたもの

The antennas around the bridge are folded piece of photo etched material.

28

艦橋の周囲に取り付けられたアンテナ。基部を折り曲げて立体的な形状となるが、複数のアンテナの角度を揃えるのは神経を使う作業

The antenna mounted around a bridge. The base is folded into a three-dimensional shape, but it is a nerve-wracking task to align the angles of multiple antennas.

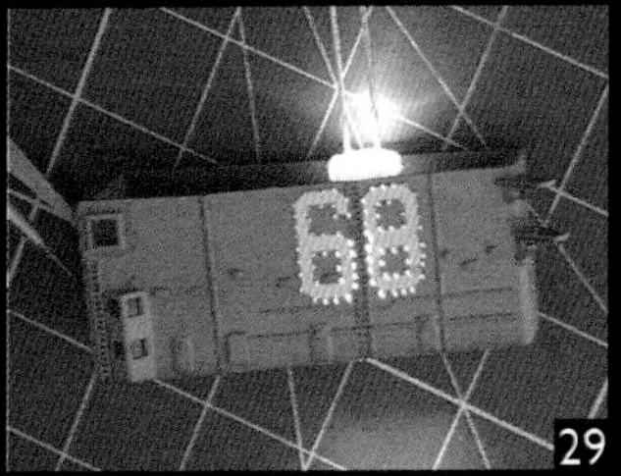

29

艦橋の"68"の電飾テスト。パーツを直に開口し裏側からLEDを当てる、という方式だが不採用。光ファイバーを収める方法を選択した

The lighting test of the "68" on the bridge. Holes are opened and optical fibers are used for the lights.

30

アンテナまでとりつけた艦橋の完成状態。電飾点灯は光漏れチェックのためだが、やはり完成させると点けたくなる、というのも大きい

A completed bridge with antennas. The lighting is done to check for light leakage.

How To Build PIT-ROAD 1/700 Scale USS Nimitz (CVN-68)

31

国旗デカールをアルミ箔に貼り乾燥後に切り出し、風にはためいている状態を再現。星条旗以外の旗は資料を確認し、汎用デカールを使用

The decal of the national flag is pasted on aluminum foil and cut out after drying to reproduce the state of flapping in the wind. Other flags are from general decal sets.

32

旗をマストに取り付けた状態。単調な色味の中でひときわ目を引く。極小サイズながらも表情をつけられた星条旗の存在感が大きい

The flag attached to a mast. It stands out among monotonous colors. Even though it is a very small size, the presence of the expressive American flag is big.

33

飛行甲板の塗装準備のためにマスキングを施した状態。デカールは使用せずにすべて塗装とする、ひたすら根気が必要な作業

Masking is applied in preparation for painting the flight deck. Painting without using decals requires a lot of patience.

34

エレベーターにも細かいパターンのラインがあるが、ここもマスキングしての塗装で塗り分ける。これで"これより塗装開始"という段階

Elevators also have fine pattern lines, which are also painted with masking. Painting begins now.

35

甲板と船体を合わせ、隙間埋めをして船体色を塗装。全部組んでから塗装ではなく、組み立て、マスキング、塗装という工程を積み重ねる

The deck and the hull are put together, and the color of the hull is painted.

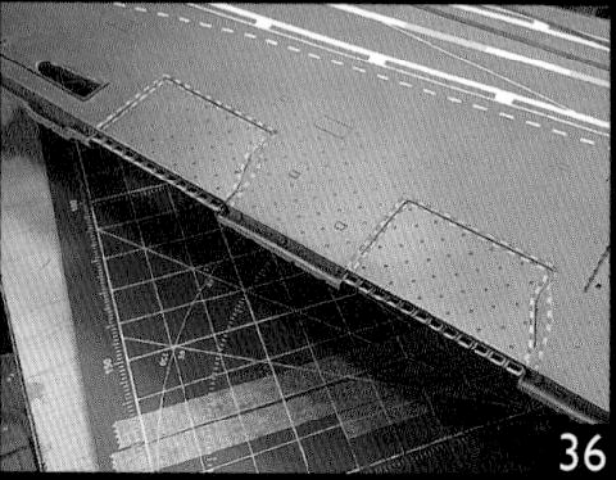

36

複雑で細いラインなので、むしろデカールをきれいに貼る方が難しいという判断からエレベーターのラインもすべてマスキングで塗り分け

Since it is a complicated and thin line, it is rather difficult to apply decal neatly. All the lines of the elevator is painted after masking.

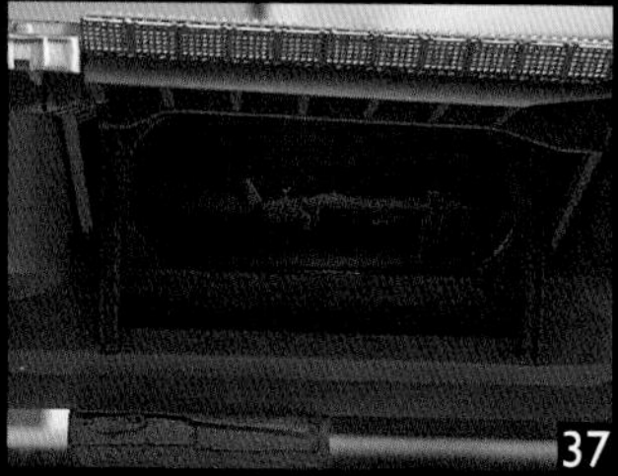

37

格納庫内にも電飾を施し点灯チェック。あえて夜間照明の赤を選択した理由は"カッコイイ"から。同時に見る者に緊張感を想起させる

The interior of the hangar is also decorated and checked. He chose red for the night lighting to create tension.

38

塗装の終わった飛行甲板に艦橋を仮置きしてみたところ。気分が盛り上がるので艦載機も並べると、モチベーションも一気に上がる

A bridge was temporarily placed on the painted flight deck wth completed aircraft.

39

飛行甲板の"縁の下の力持ち"、フォークリフトや牽引トラクターといった車両はエッチングパーツ製。ほぼ単色なので組んでから塗装

Vehicles such as forklifts and tractors are made of photo etched parts. It is almost a single color, so paint after assembling.

40

脇役ながら大きな存在感を示すのは大型クレーンを装備した6輪トラクター。これらはすべてファイブスター製のエッチングパーツ

A six-wheel tractor equipped with a large crane has a big presence. These are all photo etched parts from Five star.

41

車両関係に塗装と軽いウェザリングを行なう。基本塗装後、控え目に陰影を描くウォッシングを行なうだけで充分にメリハリが効いてくる

Coating and light weathering are applied to vehicles. After the basic coating, washg with a moderate shade.

42

コルセアⅡの試作。主翼の折り曲げ、ノズルの置換、キャノピーはヒートプレスなど、ある程度の手ごたえを感じられたので量産化に移行

Trial build of CorsairII This is with the bending of the main wing, replacement of the nozzle, and heat pressing of the canopy.

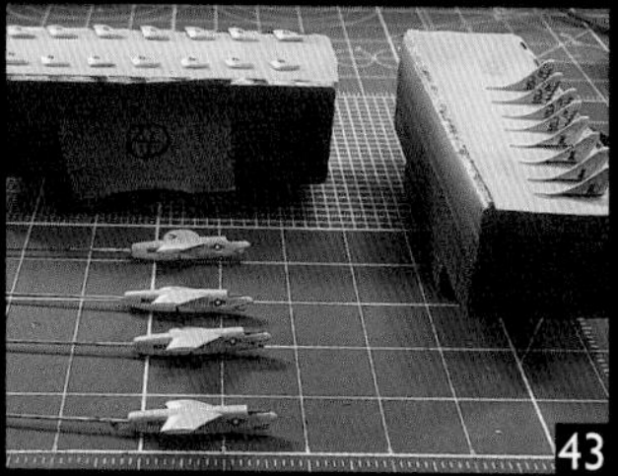

43

エンジンノズル組み付けのため、垂直尾翼も一旦カットして成型。その後、塗装とデカール貼り付けまでを行なう。写真奥に並ぶのは主翼端

To assemble the engine nozzle, the vertical tail is cut and molded. In the back of the photo are the wing tips.

44

キャノピーはヒートプレスで再現。ここから切り出し機体形状に合わせてひたすらフィッティング。ただし単なるキャノピー透明化ではない

Canopy is reproduced by heat press. From here, it is simply fitted according to the body shape. But it's not just canopy transparency.

45

甲板上でのオープン状態を再現するため、成型したキャノピーをさらに前後にカット。キャノピーフレーム部分は塗装で塗り分けている

Cut the molded canopy's front and rear to recreate the open condition on the deck. The canopy frame is painted separately.

46

資料を見ているうちに出会ったF-14のエンジン。プラ材と汎用エッチングパーツによる自作。エンジンノズルはアドラーズ・ネスト特注品

cratch build F -14 engine. Made with plastic rod and eneral-purpose photo etched parts and Adler's Nest pecial order engine nozzle.

47

エンジン単体の試作の手ごたえを経て、整備中の機体にチャレンジ。レドームを跳ね上げ、取り外したエンジンは自作台車に搭載している

After experimenting with scratch build engine, I tried to work on an aircraft under maintenance.

48

航空機模型のキモとなるエンジンノズル。発注先のアドラーズネストには機体接続部と先端の直径と全長を伝え、あとはおまかせ

The engine nozzle is the key to aircraft models. The diameter of both ends and total length are needed for Adler's Nest to create this parts.

49

主翼折り曲げ、キャノピーオープンのコルセアIIの完成。飛行甲板に並べてみた結果、「なんだか寂しい」という理由でさらに同数を製作

The Corsair II with the bent main wing and canopy open is completed. The same number of pieces were produced after testing fit on the deck.

50

次にS-3ヴァイキング。主翼はカット。機体の手前にあるのはコクピットに納めるシート。並列複座の機体なので各機2個ずつ用意した

Next is the S -3 Viking. The wing is cut. Two units o seat were prepared because of its parallel seats.

51

ヴァイキングの格納状態。主翼のみならず垂直尾翼も折り曲げる。コクピットはタガネで彫り込み、キャノピーはヒートプレス

he parking state of the viking. Not only the main wing ut also the vertical tail is bent. The cockpit is carved vith a chisel, and the canopy is heat pressed.

52

塗装とデカール貼り付けまで終了し完成したヴァイキング。よく見ると飛行前チェック用のタグが主翼からぶら下がっているのがわかる

Completed Viking after finishing painting and decal application. A closer look shows the pre-flight check tag hanging from the wing.

53

A-6イントルーダーの製作。他の機体と同様にコクピットの彫り込み、キャノピーはヒートプレス、主翼の折り畳み駐機状態を再現

A-6 intruder. Like other aircraft, the carving of the cockpit, the heat press of the canopy and the folding of the main wing are reproduced.

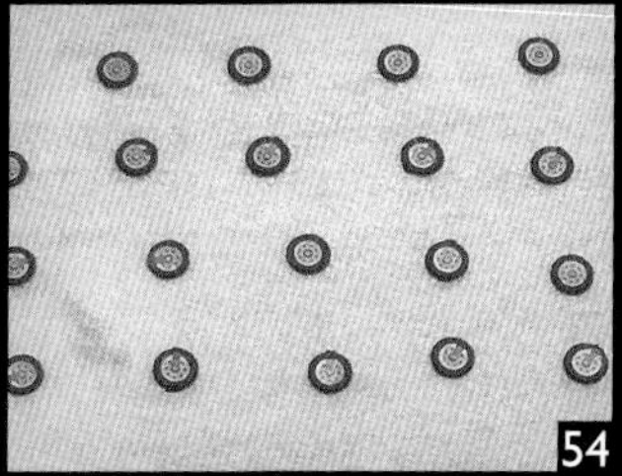

54

タイヤパーツ。右側の小さめのものがノーズギア、左の大きめのものがメインギア。ホイールとタイヤはキチンと塗り分け組み立てる

Tire parts. The small one on the right is the nose gear, and the large one on the left is the main gear.

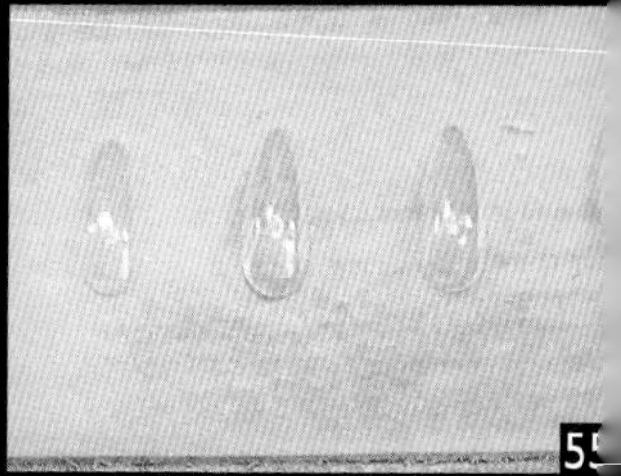

55

ヒートプレスを行なったキャノピー。多めに絞り、状態の良いものから機体へのフィッティングを行なっていく。幅は2mmほど

A heat pressed canopy. The width is about 2mm Select better parts from pile of pressed parts.

56

イントルーダーの完成。キャノピーオープンと搭乗用タラップの展開が確認できる。キャノピーグラスが塗り分けられているのもポイント

he intruder is complete. You can see the canopy pening and boarding ladders. Canopy glass is painted

57

プラウラーの製作。スジボリ堂のタガネを数種類使用してキャノピーを削除、コクピット部分を彫り込む。ほとんど失敗しない、とのこと

The production of a Prowler. The canopy is removed and the cockpit part is carved using chisel from

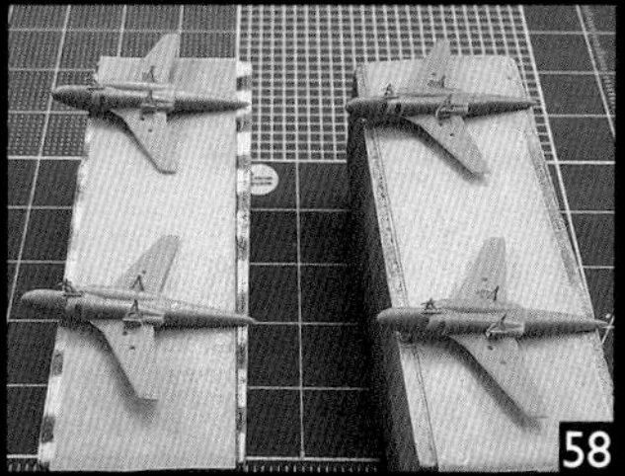

58

専用エッチングパーツによる着陸脚を組み付けた状態。垂直・水平尾翼は一旦カットして成型、塗装、デカール貼りののちに再接着

The landing gears are assembled with special etched parts. The stabilizers are cut and molded, painted, and

59

プラウラーの完成。こちらもキャノピーを跳ね上げ、搭乗用タラップを展開。タラップの赤は機体マーキングに負けないアイキャッチ

The plowler is complete. Canopy is lifted and a boarding laddar is deployed. The red paint of the

60

艦載機を仮載せ。圧倒的に数が足りないと感じ、コルセアIIとイントルーダーを各8機、プラウラーとヴァイキングを各2機ずつ追加製作した

Aircrafts are temporarily loaded. I felt that the number was insufficient, so he added 8 CorsairII and

　ピットロード製の1/700 F-14は非常に素性のいいキットで、このサイズだとどうしても気になる主翼のモールドや厚さもシャープな印象となっている。非常に小さいデカールもきれいに印刷されており、そのまま作って空母に載せても充分である。
　今回はF-14がテーマのコンペに合わせるということでさらなるディテールアップを敢行。コクピットは四角く彫り、内部にプラ材で作った極小のシートを搭載。キャノピーは透明プラ版をヒートプレスして製作したものを取り付けている。スパローやサイドワインダーといった搭載兵装は真ちゅう線で本体を作り、プラペーパーでフィンを取り付けることで自作した。さらに機体の動翼も駐機状態の機体の水平尾翼は角度を変更、発艦直前の機体はちゃんと前縁スラットとフラップが下りている状態になっているなど、非常に緻密な工作が施されている

The 1/700 F -14 from Pitroad is a very good kit to start with. The mold and thickness of the main wing, which you can't help but be concerned about, give a sharp impression. Very small decals are beautifully printed. This time, we are going to add more details by matching F -14 for the magazine's competition. The cockpit is carved into a square and has a very small seat made of plastic inside. The canopy is made by heat pressing a transparent plastic plate. The Sparrow and Side Winders are equipped with brass wires and fins attached to them. In addition, the aircraft's sweeping wing,the horizontal stabilizer of the aircraft, which are in parked position, have been altered with appropriate angle. The aircrafts just before the launch has been rigorously modified with leading edge slats and flaps down.

全体が緻密にディテールアップされた本作。F-14の他、A-7 コルセアⅡとE-2 ホークアイも全てピットロードの「1/700 現用米国空母艦載機」に付属していたものを使用した。もうひとつの本作の見所が艦内の電飾。艦橋にはグリーンのチップLEDを、船内の格納庫には夜間照明として赤色のチップLEDを搭載。船体内部に配線を這わせ、ベースの支柱を通してベース裏面の電池に接続している

Thw whole piece has a detailed look. In addition to F-14, A-7 CorsairII and E-2 Hawk-Eye were all provided with "1/700 U.S. carrier-based aircraft" by Pitroad. Another highlight of this work is the lighting system on the ship. The bridge is equipped with green chip LEDs, and the hangars on the ship are equipped with red chip LEDs for night time lighting. Wiring is made inside the hull, and it is connected to the battery on the back of the base through the support of the base.

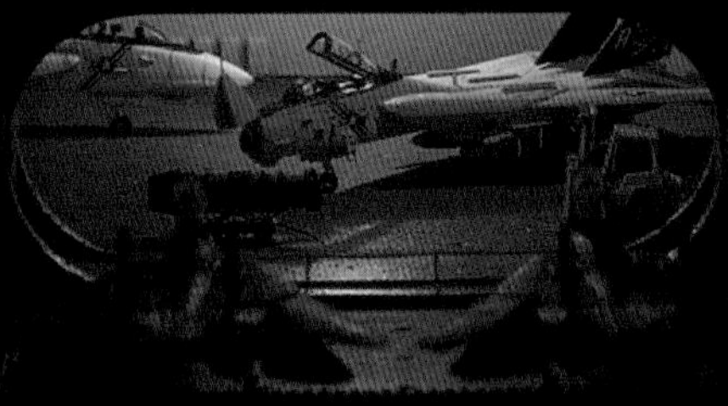

TRUMPETER 1/700 Scale Russian Navy Aircraft Carrier ADMIRAL KUZNETSOV

黒海に宿るロシア海軍の象徴、アドミラルクズネツォフ

『スケールアヴィエーション』誌上コンベンション企画のテーマ"フランカー"に合わせて製作されたアドミラル・クズネツォフ。その主役こそは飛行甲板に並ぶSu-35たち。黒のドレスをまとった貴婦人、クズネツォフがそれらの機体を最高に引き立てる

Admiral Kuznetsov was created according to the theme "flanker" of the convention on the Scale Aviation magazine. The main characters are the Su -35s on the flight deck. Kuznetsov, a lady in a black dress, brings out the best look of them.

ロシア海軍航空母艦 アドミラル・クズネツォフ
トランペッター１／700 インジェクションプラスチックキット

TRUMPETER 1/700 Russian Navy Aircraft Carrier ADMIRAL KUZNETSOV
Injection-plastic kit

アドミラルクズネツォフとは

浮かんでは消えるを繰り返した旧ソ連の空母建造計画の中で、唯一、本格的な空母として完成したのがアドミラル・クズネツォフ級の2隻である。ご存じのように２番艦「ヴァリャーグ」は曲折を経て中国海軍の手に渡り、現在は「遼寧」になっている。したがって、現在、ロシア海軍に残るのはネームシップの１隻だけである。

ロシア海軍の空母保有計画は常に野心的であったが、いずれも政変や莫大な建造費用見積もりを前に挫折した。そこで1979年に計画が始動した本級では、原子力推進や蒸気カタパルトといった高額設備をあきらめ、スキージャンプ式とした５万トン級の通常動力型空母という現実的な計画によって完成にこぎ着けた。 しかし完成とソ連崩壊がほぼ同時であった影響で稼働率は極めて低く、特に前半世はほぼ放置された状態のまま艦齢が30年を迎えてしまった。2016年には初の実戦任務としてシリア内戦に投入されて存在感を見せつけたものの、航行中に黒煙を吹くなど機関部の不調も明らかで、2017年には全面的な近代化改修工事に入っているとのこと。再就役は2021年とされているが、いよいよ退役も現実味を帯びてきたようだ

Of the former Soviet plans to build an aircraft carrier, only two Admiral-Kuznetsov-class aircraft carriers were completed. As you know, the 2nd vessel "Varyag" was handed over to the PLAN after many twists and turns, and is now called the "Liaoning". Therefore, only the name ship remains in the Russian Navy.The Russian Navy's plans to possess aircraft carriers hThus, this class, which plan was started in 1979, gave up expensive such as nuclear propulsion and steam catapult, and was completed by a realistic plan of a 50,000 ton class conventional powered aircraft carrier with a ski jump style launching deck. However, the operating rate was very low because the completion of the ship was almost at the same time as the collapse of the Soviet Union, and in particular, the first half of its 30 year history, the ship was untouched and almost abandoned. The ship made its presence felt during the Syrian civil war in 2016 when it was deployed for the first time as part of a combat mission, but it is also reported that malfunctions of its engine, as blowing black smoke during cruising, were evident, and in 2017, the entire ship was undergoing repair and modernization. Admiral Kuznetsov is expected to be reassigned in 2021, but retirement seems to be becoming a reality.

КУЗМЕЦОВ

063

このクズネツォフもまた
フランカーを魅力的に見せるための展示台

旧帝国海軍艦船の模型製作を主戦場としている笹原にとってロシア海軍、それも現用艦船の製作は、当然ながら普段とは勝手の違うことの連続であり、そもそも1／700スケールのフランカー完成の目処が立たなければ製作に踏み切るつもりはなかったという。現用空母は、トムキャットのベースとして製作したニミッツ以来2年ぶり、2作目となるが、クズネツォフもニミッツ同様、フランカーのベースとしての製作だ。甚だ豪華すぎるベースであるが、そこは艦船模型界の雄、悪役感溢れるロシアンビューティを見事なクオリティで仕上げている。

製作においては前述のように、そもそも現用艦のディテールのおさらいや使用可能なエッチングパーツの取捨選択など時間的なロスも多いという。くわえてクズネツォフのキット付属のフランカーはクリア成型の為、細工が困難。あらゆる方策を経て、トランペッターの遼寧に付属するフランカー(正しくはJ - 15) と専用エッチングパーツを入手することで成形色、ディテールともに製作に踏み切ることができたという。フランカーありきのクズネツォフ、という立ち位置は変わらないのだ。キット自体は少々古いこともあってパーツの合いなど基本工作で苦労させられたものの、艦橋周りてんこ盛りのレーダーやセンサーなどのディテールは新鮮で面白みがあり、また「この古い船体でよく持ってるなぁ」と楽しみながら製作できたという。

船体の塗装については、資料をあたる上で濃淡2パターンのグレーが確認できたが、ここはやはり悪役チックな濃いグレーの船体をチョイス。また完成を前にして格納庫内が真っ暗であることに気付き、こちらもニミッツ以来の電飾加工を施し、格納庫内の機体にもスポットライトを当てている。■

For Sasahara, who is mainly engaged in the production of models of the former Imperial Japanese Navy vessels, the production of the Russian Navy, and of modern naval vessels, was naturally a series of unusual things and he did not intend to produce them unless he could foresee the completion of a 1/700 scale franker. Kuznetsov, is a second modern aircraft carrier like Nimitz for Sasahara, is a base for the flanker. It is an extremely luxurious base, but he, the masters in the ship modeling world, finishes this Russian beauty with an impressive quality.

As mentioned above, there is a lot of time loss in manufacturing, such as reviewing details of the current ship and selection of usable photo etched parts. In addition, the flanker that comes with Kuznetsov's kit is clear parts so it is difficult to work and modify. After taking every possible measure, he obtained a flanker (J-15) attached to trumpeter's "Liaoning" kit and special etching parts and enabled to start both the coloring and the detailing of the molds. Kuznetsov's position as a flanker's exhibition stand is unchanged. Since the kit itself was a little old,it was difficult to do basic work such as fitting the parts, but the radar and sensors around the bridge were interesting, and it was very enjoyable build. As for the painting of the hull, he could confirm two shades of gray patterns when we checked the documents, but he chose a dark gray for the hull for a more evil look. Before it was completed, he noticed that the inside of the hangar was completely dark, therefor he used the same lighting process that he had used on Nimitz to light the inside of its hangar.

甲板上に並ぶフランカー、その主翼は発進位置についた展開状態のものだけでなく、折りたたんだ格納状態、そして発進位置に向かう展張途中の状態と、じつに動きのある様を見せている。これらは製作当初から明確なビジョンとして頭の中にあるのではなく、資料とした動画などを見ているうちに「こういった動きを加えたほうが面白いな、カッコイイな」と考えてのことだという。機体背面で展開状態のエアブレーキや発艦位置のディフレクター裏面のディテールはエッチングパーツによるものだが、これらを歪みなく丁寧に配することで、わずか3cmほどの機体に命が宿るのだ

The flankers on the deck. The main wings are not only in the deployed state, but in the retracted position and also in the spreading state toward the launching position. Showing many realistic movements. Sasahara didn't have a clear vision in his mind from the beginning, but he thought "It's interesting and cool to add this kind of movement." while watching the reference videos. The details of the air brakes deployed in the back of the fuselage and the deflector on the launch location deck are built with photo etched parts, by carefully arranging them without distortion, the life is given to three-centimeter-long fuselage.

SAコンベンションのお題を聞いた時点では「自分の出る幕はないな」と考えていたが、編集部からフランカーでの参加を打診され、検討を開始。クズネツォフ付属のフランカーはクリア成型の為、いつものように細かい細工を加えることができなかった。ピットロードの1/700ロシア機セットのフランカーは発売時期を踏まえるとディテール的に厳しく、頼みの綱とばかりに入手したトランペッターの遼寧に付属する機体とエッチングパーツがあったからこそ、SAコン参加の第一段階をクリアしたという。次なるステップはフランカーの特徴的な洋上迷彩の再現。ここで笹原自身が納得のいくクオリティで迷彩塗装ができると判った時点で、ようやくクズネツォフを（フランカーのベースとして）製作する判断に至った。フランカーの塗装は1/700サイズながらいつも通り、エアブラシによるもの。ごく薄く濃度調整された塗料を艦船の製作と同様、ひたすらマスキングとエアブラシ塗装を丁寧に繰り返すことで、このとんでもなく精緻な空間が生まれる。己のフィールドとは異なる現用艦船。「もう現用艦はこりごり」と笹原は言うが、新たなチャレンジを見たい、とクズネツォフを見た誰もが感じることだろう

When he heard the topic of the SA-CON, his thought was "Its not my turn." but the editorial office asked him to participate with franker build, so he started to consider to be a part of it. The flanker attached to Kuznetsov was not able to add fine workmanship as usual because of the clear parts molding. The flanker for the 1/700 Russian plane set from Pitroad was very low in detail because the time of the release. The first stage of participation in the SA-con passed with Flanker from trumpeter kit and available photo etched parts for the flanker. The next step is to reproduce the characteristic camouflage of the flanker
When Sasahara realized that camouflage painting was possible with great quality, he finally decided to produce Kuznetsov (As the base for flankers). The flanker is painted with the usual airbrush, although it is 1/700 size. Just as in the painting of the ship, a very thin paints are used. Carefully repeat masking and airbrush painting to create this incredibly detailed surface. "I have had enough of the Modern ship." says Sasahara, but anyone who sees Kuznetsov will feel and want to see a his new challenge.

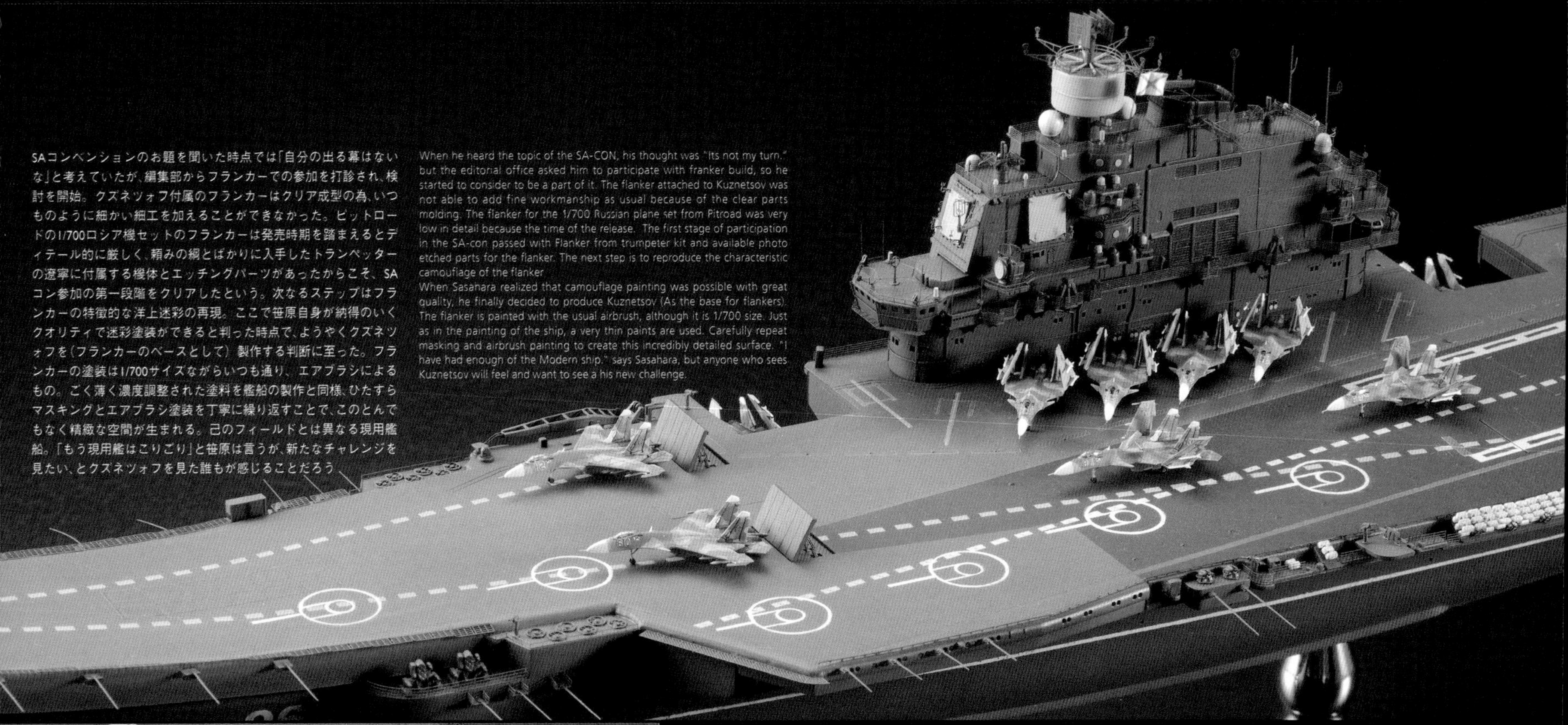

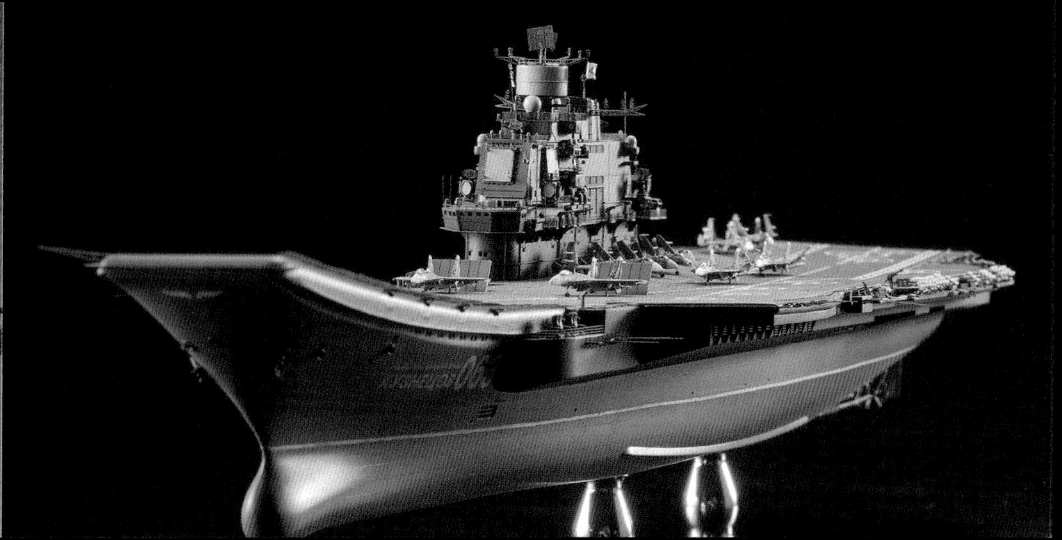

How To Build TRUMPETER 1/700 Scale Russian Navy Aircraft Carrier ADMIRAL KUZNETSOV

1

クズネツォフはパーツの嵌合が悪かったので、まず船体上下を接着して接合部を処理。あわせて全体にヤスリを掛け、ヒケ処理も行なった

Since the parts of Kuznetsov did not fit well, the upper and lower parts of the hull were first glued and the joint was filed. At the same time, sink marks treated.

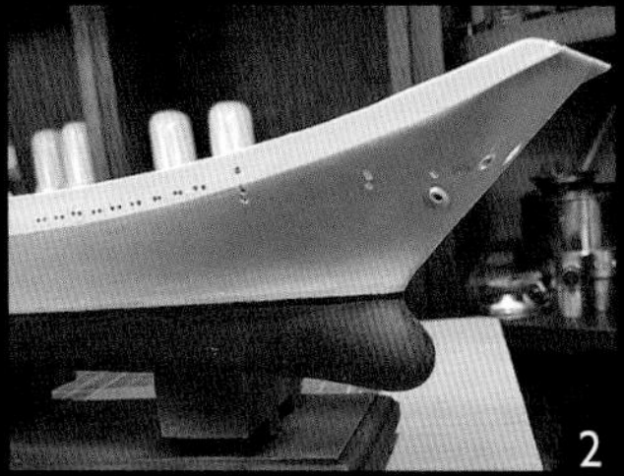

2

この特徴的な船首の形状がクズネツォフの魅力のひとつ。写真資料と突き合わせ、ディテールやフォルムの差異を入念にチェックする

This characteristic shape of the bow is one of the charms of Kuznetsov. Match with photo materials and carefully check for differences in details and form.

3

艦尾側面の構造物。パーツ同士の嵌合の悪さは全体に及んでおり、ここでも隙間にパテを充てんしたり、延ばしランナーで埋めたりしている

The structure on the stern side of a ship. The poor fit between the parts is everywhere, and again, the gaps are filled with putty or sprunners.

4

吸気口は開口して裏側からメッシュを取り付ける。メッシュのサイズなどはそれらしいものを汎用エッチングパーツよりチョイスしてきた

The air inlet is opened, and the mesh is installed from the rear side. The size of the mesh has been chosen from general etching parts.

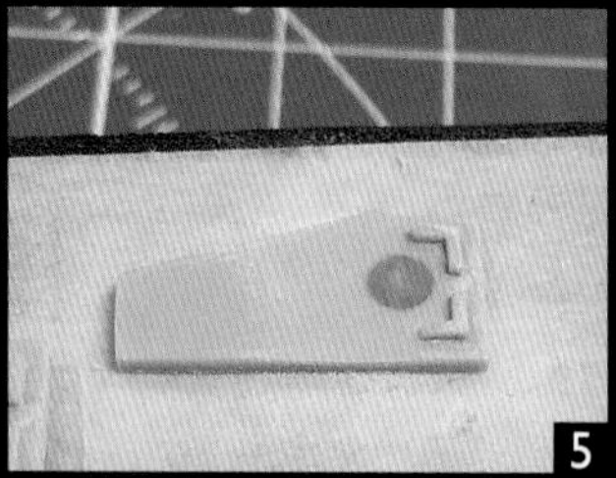

5

パーツ裏面のイジェクトピン跡など目立つ箇所はすべてパテなど処理している。どう処理すれば完成までが近いか、を考えつつ作業していく

All conspicuous spots such as ejection pin marks on the back side of the parts are treated with putty.

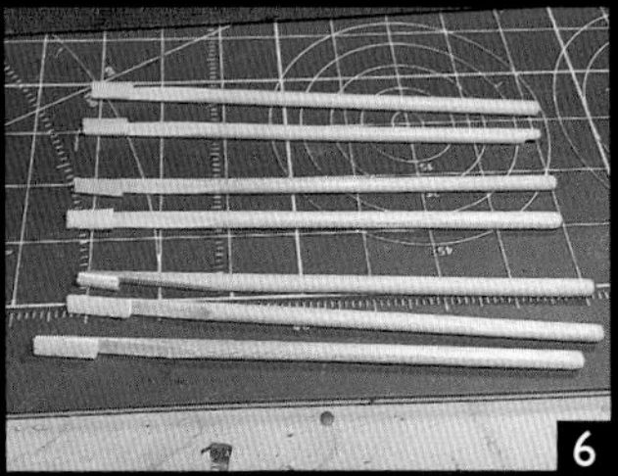

6

必要に応じてツールも自作する。細部削り用の爪楊枝ヤスリは、耐水ペーパーをプラ板に貼り爪楊枝の先端に接着した。番手は600番と800番

Create your own tools as needed. For the toothpick file for fine sanding is sand paper stuck to the plastic plate and glued to the tip of the toothpick. The grit size are 800 and 600.

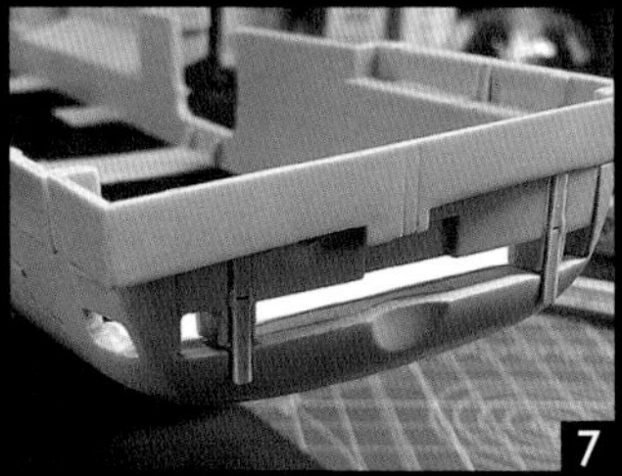

7

艦尾の開口部内はかなりパテのお世話になるため、爪楊枝ヤスリは、まさにこういった細く奥まった箇所の仕上げに重宝する

The opening of the stern is modified with putty, so the toothpick file is very useful for finishing such narrow, deep parts.

8

キットは、各部のディテールが開口していたり凹表現のみであったりとバラバラ。またきちんと水平が出ていない箇所も散見される

The details of each part of the kit had different expression. There are also places where the horizontal line does not come out properly.

9

あまりにズレたディテールなどは一旦、プラ材で埋めて、再度正確な位置に開口したりディテールを彫り込んだ方がきれいに仕上がる

If there are too many misaligned details, it will look better if you fill them with plastic sheet and re-open them in the correct position or engrave details.

10

吸気口周辺の白い箇所はプラ材。資料と異なるディテールやヒケの修正を行なった。吸気口の開口はピンバイスとヤスリ、タガネで追い込む

The white area around the inlet is made of plastic sheet. The wrong details were corrected. The opening of the air inlet is made by a pin vice, file, and chisel.

11

吸気口に汎用エッチングパーツのメッシュを貼り込む。開口部の加工は、慌てず丁寧に作業を行なえばパーツの破損はほとんど発生しない

Attach the mesh from a general purpose etching part set to the inlet. When working on the opening, if you work carefully, the damage to the part will hardly occur.

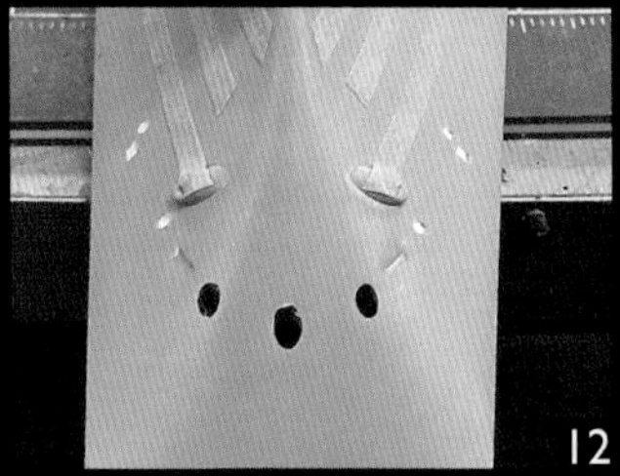

12

クズネツォフの特徴である、船体の鉄板溶接痕を再現するため、等間隔でマスキングテープを貼り込み準備をしておく

In order to reproduce the steel plate welding mark of the hull, which is a characteristic of Kuznetsov, masking tape is applied at equal intervals and preparation is done.

13

艦首部は丸穴を開口してハトメを取り付ける。とくに模型用の製品ではなく、一般的に流通しているハトメ製品からサイズを選択して使用

A round hole is opened at the bow to install the eyelet. It is not a modeling product in particular, but is used by selecting a size from commonly available eyelet products.

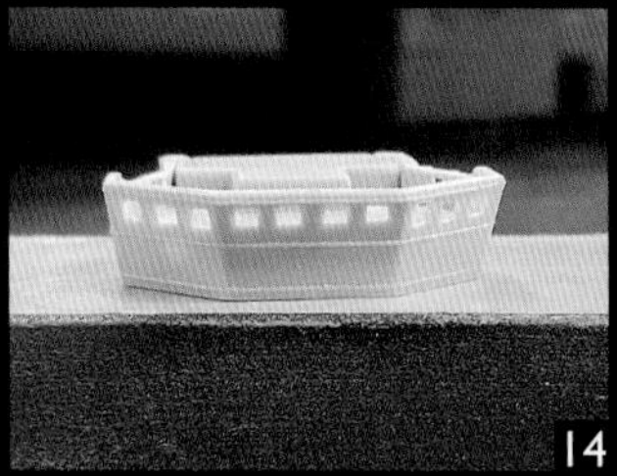

14

本作では艦橋の電飾は行なわないので透明プラ板は使用せず窓部分はすべて開口。角をキチンとシャープに処理するとスケール感が向上する

In this work, there won't be any lighting decoration of the bridge. All windows are open but no transparent sheet is used. Sharpening the corners improve the sense of scale.

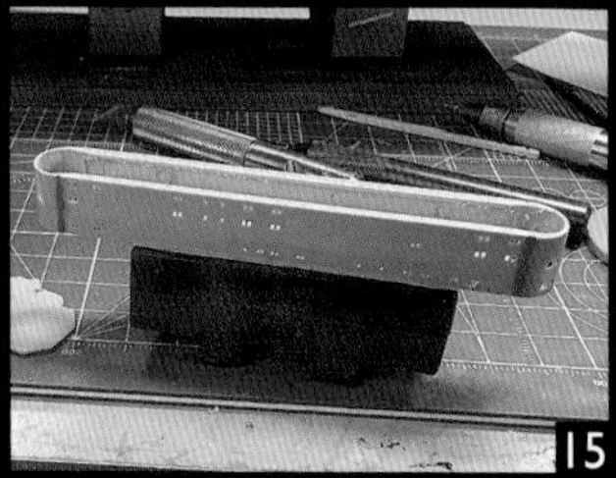

15

艦橋一層部はパーツの合わせ目処理をパテにて行なった。天井部のダボ穴は不要なため、ここもパテで平滑になるよう処理している

For the first layer of the bridge, the joint processing of the parts was carried out with putty. Since the dowel holes on the ceiling are unnecessary, they are also made smooth by putty.

16

一層部の穴はもともと開口されているが、大きさが揃っていない。タガネやヤスリを用いてサイズと形状を整えた

The holes in the first layer are open originally, but are not uniform in size. Shaped and size was corrected with files.

17

一層部の穴は、一部はプラ材を用いて一旦埋めてから穴をきれいに開け直している。ところどころ白く見える部分がプラ材で修正した個所

The holes in the first layer are partially filled and then redrilled. The white parts are corrected with plastic sheet.

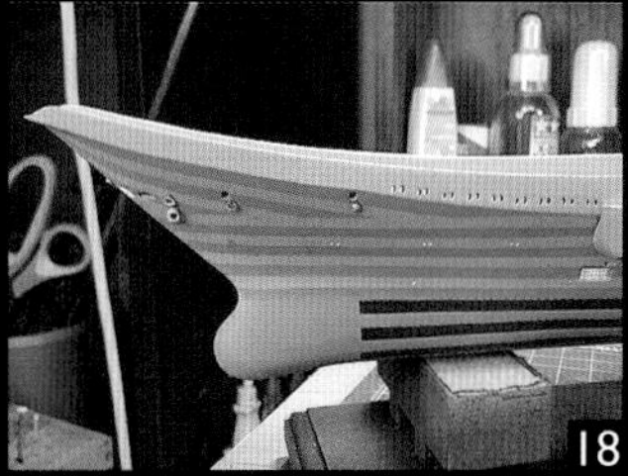

18

船体にマスキングテープを貼り、サーフェイサーを厚めに吹き付ける。乾燥後にテープをはがすと船体溶接痕の段差が表現される

A masking tape is applied to the hull and the surfacer is sprayed thickly. When the tape is peeled off after drying, the level difference will act as the hull weld mark.

19

キットではシャッターも開口されエレベーターも降下位置で組み立てられるのだが、格納庫そのものは再現されていないため、プラ板で自作

In the kit, the shutter is opened and the elevator is assembled in the descending position, but the hangar itself is not reproduced, so it was made by plastic sheet.

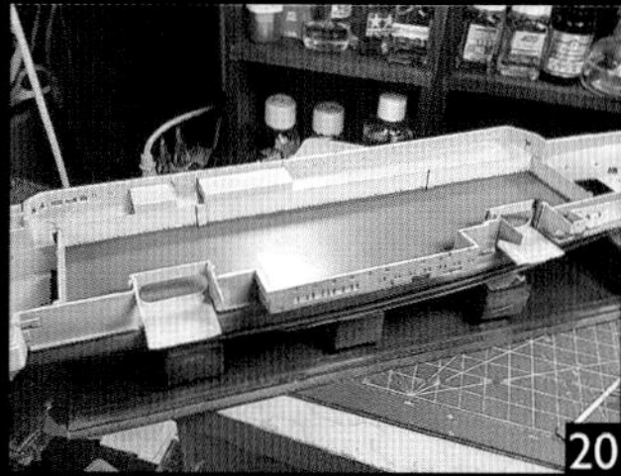

20

格納庫内のフロア面を塗装。写真を参考に独特のグリーンを調色している。西側の航空母艦ではあまり目にしない色味が新鮮

The floor of the hangar was painted. The unique green color is adjusted referring to the actual picture. The color that you don't often see on the western aircraft carrier.

21

エレベーター付近のディテールは専用エッチングパーツが未発売のため、遼寧用エッチングパーツを流用して製作している

As for the details around the elevator, photo etching parts have not yet been released, so they are made using the etching parts for Liaoning.

22

前部エレベーター周辺のディテール。黄色い部分はパテ。資料をチェックし、遼寧と異なるディテール箇所は修正を加えていく

Details around the front elevator. The yellow part is patty. I will check the documents and correct the details that are different from the Liaoning.

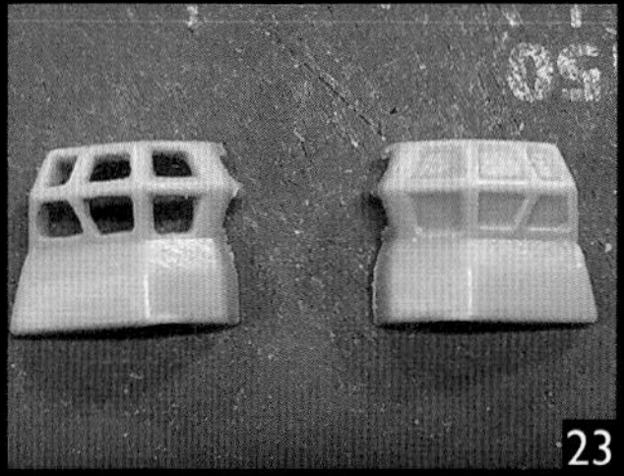

23

艦橋にある着艦指示室はパーツの左右張り合わせで独特な台形の窓のディテールを再現している。この窓もすべて開口していく

A unique shaped window of the landing instruction room on the bridge was reproduces in detail by fitting two parts together All these windows are opened.

24

左右のパーツを貼り合わせ成型し、窓を開口した状態。これを取り付ける艦橋とは入念なすり合わせを行なっておく

A landing instruction room with a window opened at 23. Left and right parts are glued together and shaped. Attaching to the bridge carefully.

25

煙突のトップ部分。キットのままでは完全にふさがった状態。どこを切除し、どのようにディテールを再現するかプランニングする

The top part of a chimney. The kit part is completely close up. Plan where to cut and how to replicate the details.

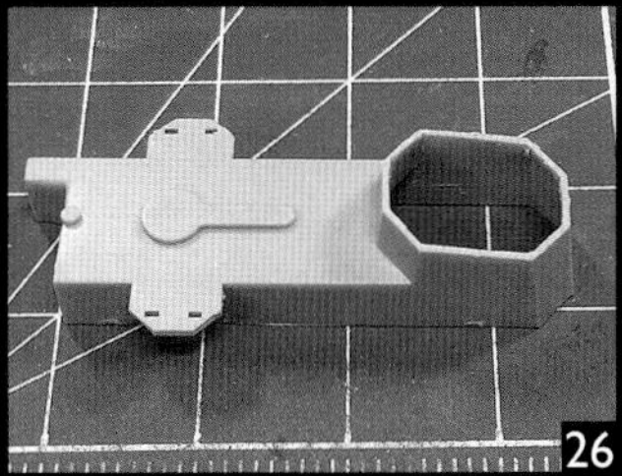

26

トップの放射状のリブを切除し、煙突の8角形を開口。フチ部分の肉厚が均一になるよう注意しながら開口部を丁寧に仕上げていく

The top radial rib was cut and make a octagon shape hole of the chimney. Carefully finish the opening while

27

詳細な資料が見つからなかったので、プラ材で放射状のリブを再現。奥にメッシュを貼り込んでそれらしいディテールをデコレート

I couldn't find any detailed information, so I reproduced the radial ribs with plastic sheet. Decorate the details

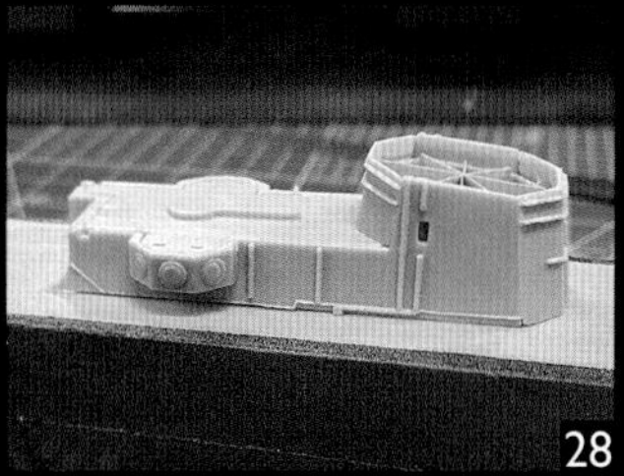

28

資料を参照しながら側面部分にディテールパーツを貼り込んでいく。パーツを基準にして垂直や平行に気をつけて精度を維持する

Paste the detail parts on the side while referring to the document. Maintain accuracy by careful placement of

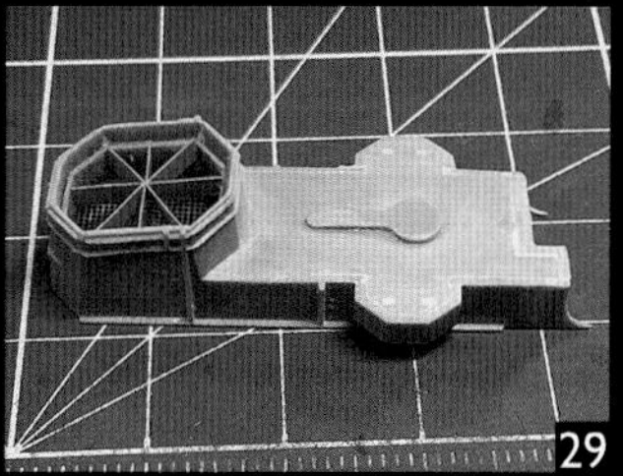

29

パーツ表面のダボ穴などはエッチングパーツなどを使用する関係上、不要となるのでパテで埋め平滑に仕上げておく

The dowel hole on the surface of the part is not necessary because of the use of the etching part, so fill

30

艦橋のトップに配置されるレーダードーム。ディテールをエッチングパーツに置換するため、不要なディテールの切除と穴埋めをする

The radar dome is located at the top of the bridge. Remove and fill in unnecessary detail to replace with an

エッチングパーツへの置換を鑑みて、キットパーツの不要なディテールと、残しておくべきディテールを見極める

Identify the unnecessary details of the kit part and the details that should be retained, considering the replacement with the photo etched part.

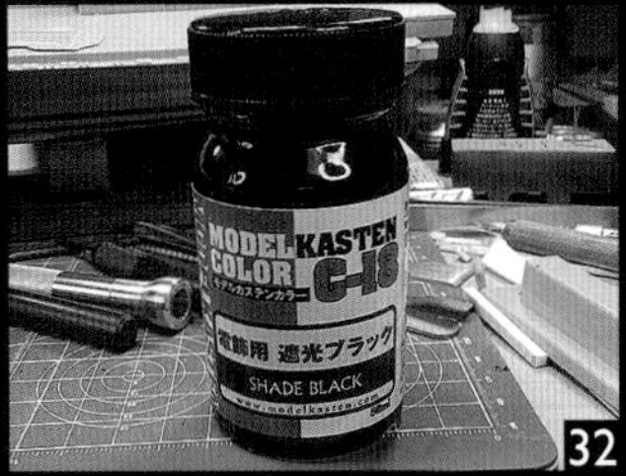

本作では電飾を行なったため、パーツの光透け防止にモデルカステンのオリジナルカラー『電飾用遮光ブラックPRO』を使用している

In this work, "Shade Black PRO" from modelkasten is used to prevent the light from being seen through some parts.because of the lighting decoration.

塗り分け作業が大変なレーダー。エッチングパーツはあらかじめ塗装しておき、各パーツも塗装しながら組み立てていく

Radar that is hard to paint. Paint the etching parts in advance, and other parts are painted while assembling.

煙突基部も塗装を済ませ、エッチングパーツのアンテナなどを取り付けた状態。アンテナの垂直には充分に留意する

The funnel base has also been painted, and the photo etched part for the antenna has been installed. Pay careful attention to the angle of the antenna.

それぞれ塗装と仕上げを済ませた煙突基部にレーダーを組み付け完成。この状態でも再度、アンテナなどの水平・垂直を入念にチェック

Radar is installed at the bottom of funnel after painting and finishing. Even at this state, check the horizonta and vertical angle of the antenna carefully again.

友人のメルパパ氏が製作したチョッパー。各部ディテールに使用するような、細いプラ材の切り出しに非常に重宝している

Chopper made by my friend Melpapa. It is very useful for cutting out thin plastic materials like those used for each part detail.

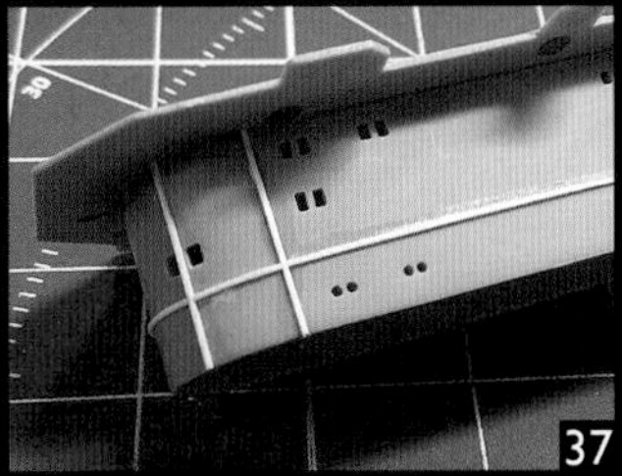

艦橋外周部のディテールの再現。第一段階は一旦キットのディテールを削り落としてから、プラ材で再生した

Th circumferencee reproduction of the details of the outer circumference of the bridge. The first step was to scrape off the details of the kit before rebuild it with plastic materials.

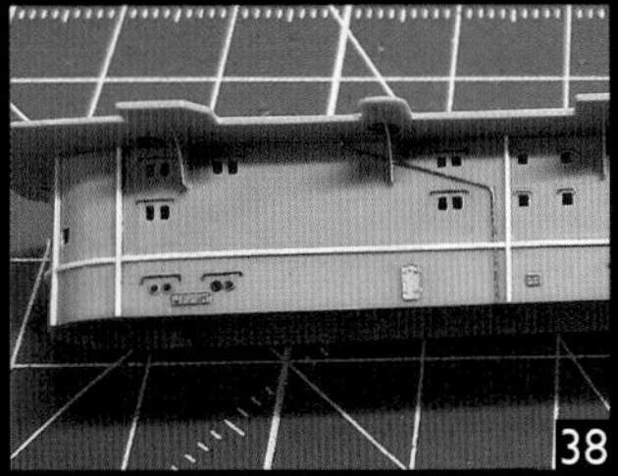

さらに窓枠などをエッチングパーツでディテールアップ。汎用エッチングパーツセットからそれらしいものをそれらしく使用

In addition, the window frame and other details are improved with photo etched parts. Use something that fits from a generic etch part set.

艦橋の上段を載せてディテールなどをチェック。ドアや梯子といったディテールは汎用エッチングパーツで再現。黒い部分が着艦指示室

Check out the details by putting the upper part of the bridge. Details such as doors and ladders are reproduced with etching parts. The black part is the landing direction room.

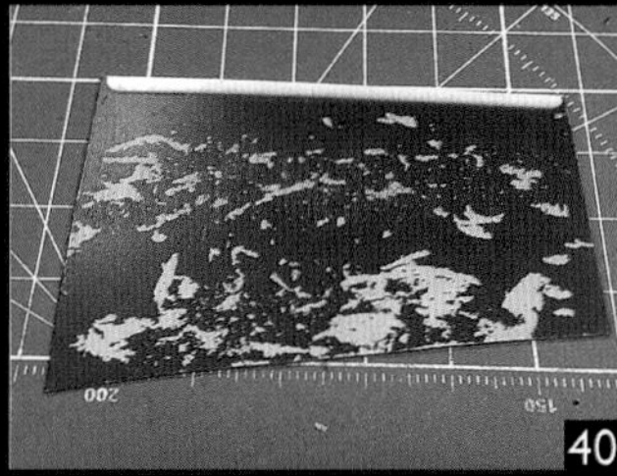

クズネツォフの特徴のひとつが艦首部分の塗装ダメージ。剥がし技法での再現をテストしたが全体の仕上がりを勘案して今回は見送った

One of the features of Kuznetsov is the paint damage on the bow. He tried to reproduce it with the peeling technique, but didn't apply it this time considering the overall finish.

各種レーダー関係のディテールアップには現用ロシア海軍汎用エッチングパーツセットを用いている。写真は塗装前の段階

The Modern Russian Navy general purpose etching part set is used for the detail up of various radars. The

キットのパーツをベースに消火栓をディテールアップ。放水銃の砲身は真ちゅうパイプに置換、汎用エッチングパーツでそれらしく仕上げた

Based on the kit parts, the fire hydrant is refined. The barrel of the water gun was replaced with brass pipes,

レーダーの塗り分けはこのサイズでもマスキングを行なう。万が一破損しても「もともと壊れて当然」くらいの気持ちで修理する

The radar is also masked even in this size. If it is damaged, repair it with the care.

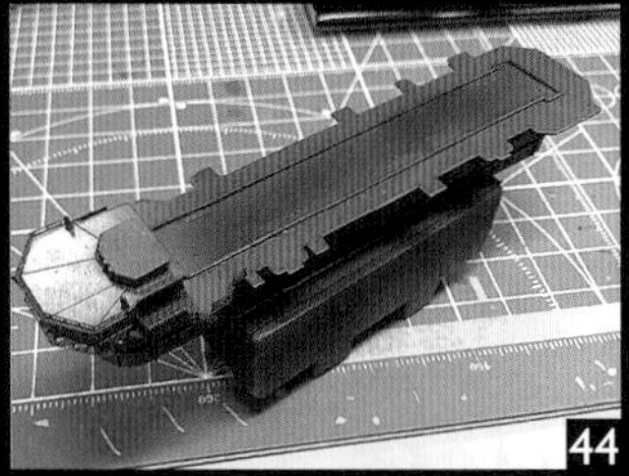

手摺の下にある床面は、手摺と同色の船体色となるよう0.2mmほどフチを残してマスキング。床と手摺の色の繋がりが自然になる

The bottom of the handrail is masked with a border of about 0.2mm. It has a effect of natural connection of

レーダーを設置し手摺も中腹まで取り付けた状態。マスキングと塗装、組み立てを繰り返すことで、この精緻な塗り分けが完成される

The radar is installed and the handrail is attached up to midway. By repeating masking, painting, and assembly,

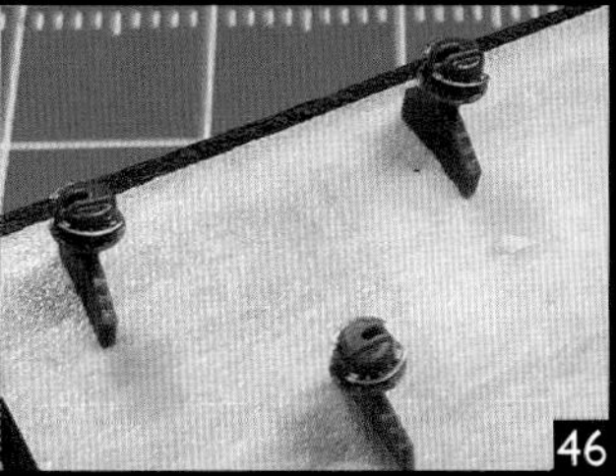
46

対空機銃は、レジン製のロシア汎用パーツを見つけたので使用してみた。ディテールは良好だが残念ながら流通在庫が見つからない状況

I used found an Russian antiaircraft gun in general-purpose part made of resin. The details are good, but unfortunately we cannot find the distribution stock.

47

ロケットランチャーのディテールアップ。右がキット、左はランチャー部を真ちゅうパイプに置き換えたもの。効果は一目瞭然

The adding more details of the rocket launcher. On the right is a kit, and on the left is a brass pipe replacing the launcher. The effect is obvious.

48

各部のアンテナも取り付け完成した艦橋。暗い船体色と対称的な赤のコントラストに、レーダーのホワイトグレーがアイキャッチとなる

The bridge is complete with antennas. The contrast between the dark hull color and the symmetrical red, and the white gray of the radar are eye-catching.

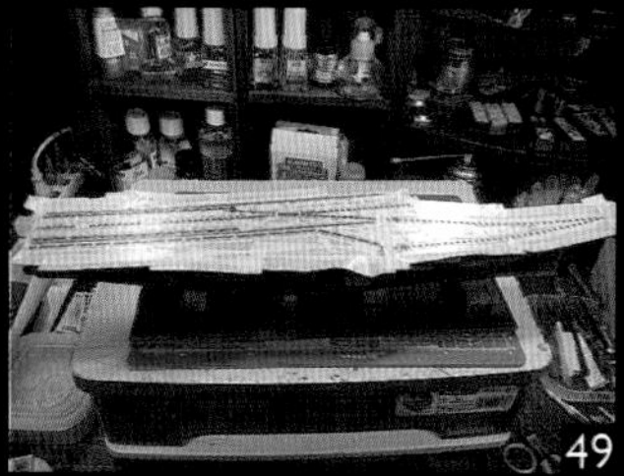
49

飛行甲板はデカールを使用せずにマスキング塗装を選択。米軍の航空母艦に較べると甲板のラインはシンプルで作業量も少ない

The flight deck was painted with masking. Compared to U.S. aircraft carriers, the deck line is simple and requires less work.

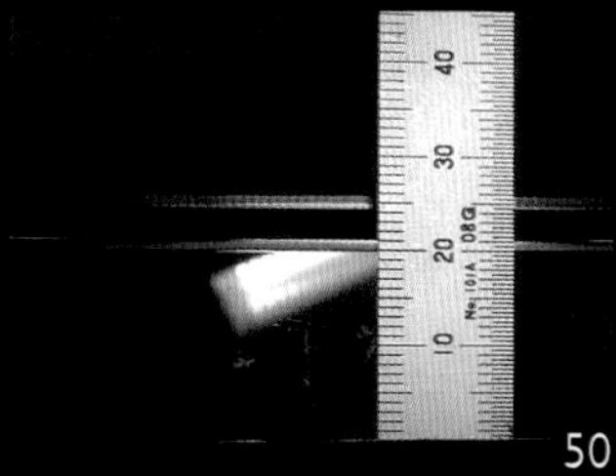
50

展示用ベースはすべて特注品。電飾を仕込む場合は立ち上げ部分を高めにし、内部を空洞にすることで電源などを仕込む

All display bases are custom made. In the case of placing electric decorations, the raised part is made higher, and the inside is made hollow, so that the power source, etc. is placed.

51

特製の塗装ブースは現用航空母艦の船体が余裕で収まる。デカールを貼ってウェザリング、デカール保護用のツヤ消しクリアーを全体に吹く

The special paint booth can accommodate the hull of Modern aircraft carrier. Apply decals then weathering. Cover the hull with Matte clear to protect decals.

52

船体に艦橋とアンテナを設置。概ね完成が見えてきた段階。あらためて色彩的な面白さと立体映えを感じる艦船である

A bridge and antenna are installed on the hull. The work is almost complete. It is a ship with an interesting sense of color and three-dimensional appearance.

53

各翼を折り畳み、コクピットを彫り込んで特注品のエンジンノズルに置換したシーフランカーの試作。パイロンや脚は専用エッチングパーツ

A test build of a sea flanker, in which each wing is folded and a cockpit is carved to replaced with a custom-made engine nozzle. Pylon and legs are specially etched parts.

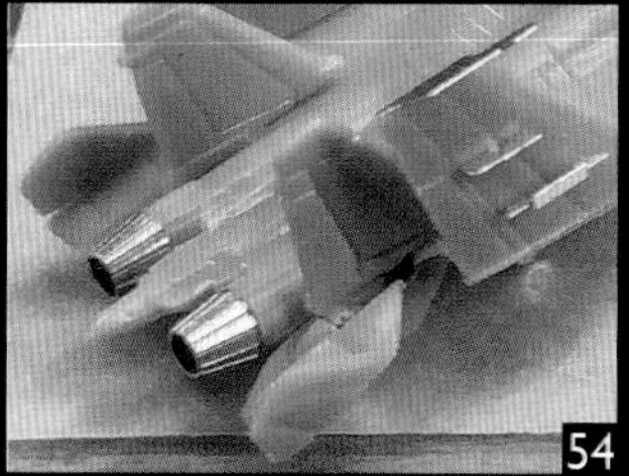
54

エンジンノズルは友人の拳王氏作の特注品。直径と長さの寸法を伝えただけで、設計まで含めてオーダー、期待を裏切らない完成度

The engine nozzle was custom-made by my friend, Ken Wang. The size of the diameter and the length are needed, and the degree of completion, including the design is perfect.

55

エアブレーキ展開状態の機体も製作。エアブレーキ部を削り込み、ブレーキ板はクセをつけたプラペーパーによるもの

An aircraft with air brakes deployed was also manufactured. The air brake part is shaved, and the brake plate is made of a bented plastic paper.

56

甲板にシーフランカーを設置。制空迷彩の青と武装の白、赤い星が際立った存在感を主張する。ヘリも並べたかったがタイムアップ

Sea flankers are installed on the deck. The blue camouflage, the white weapons, and the red star are present outstanding atmosphere.

57

クズネツォフ完成状態。レーダーはじめ艦橋構造物の現代的なデザインとスキージャンプ式飛行甲板というミスマッチ感が大きな魅力

uznetsov is complete. The modern design of radar and other bridge structures and the mismatched ski-jump deck are a major attractionof this ship.

TRUMPETER 1/700 Scale
Russian Navy Aircraft Carrier ADMIRAL KUZNETSOV

TRUMPETER 1/700 Scale
PLA Navy Aircraft Carrier Liao Ning

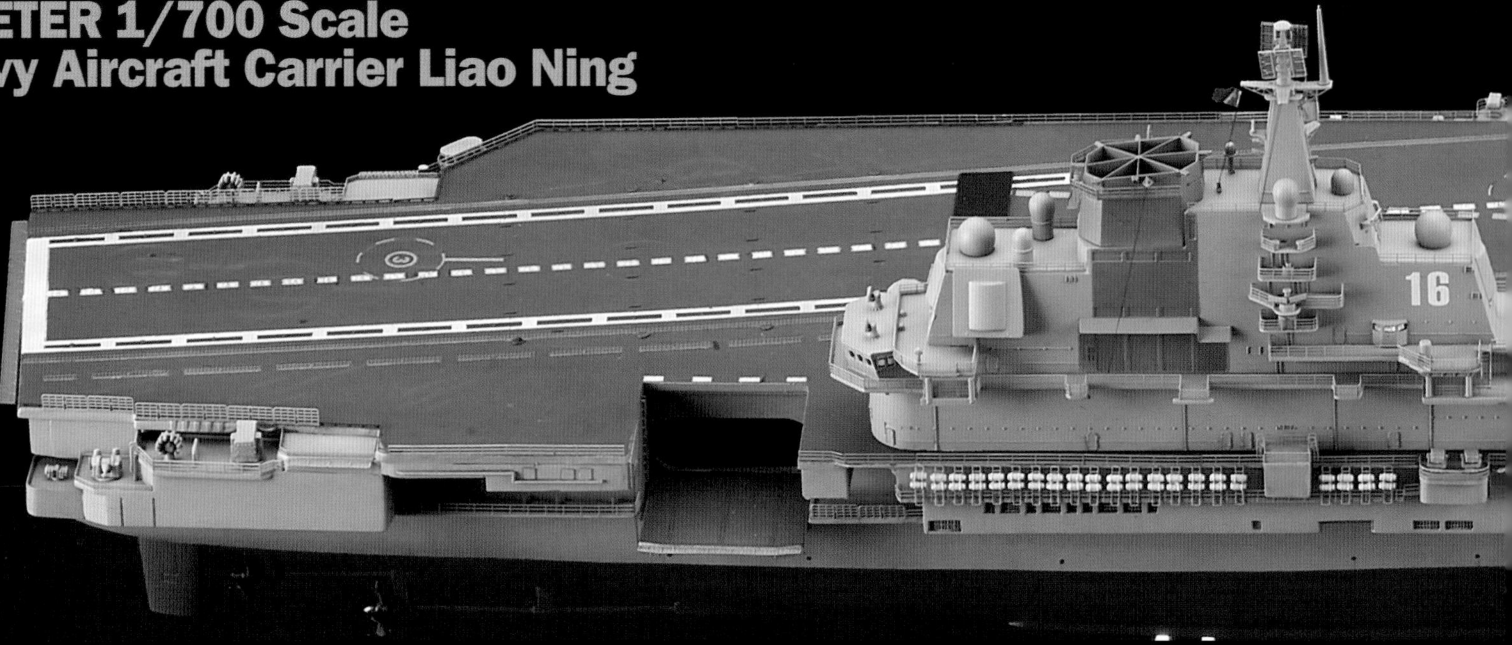

ソ連生まれの中国空母、その端正な佇まいを建造する

これまでニミッツなどの現用航空母艦を製作してきた笹原氏。その製作テーマはつねに"1/700スケール艦載機のための展示用台座"というものであった。本作でもそのポジションは変わらない。戦闘機J-15のためだけに、艦船単品であっても遜色のない高密度なディテールを盛り込んだ"本気の展示台"の雄姿がここにある

Sasahara's Modern aricraft carriers always has been an "Exhibition pedestal for 1/700 scale carrier-based aircraft". The position is the same in this work. Just for the J- -15 fighter, there is a magnificent work for the "serious display stand" which incorporates high-density details that are comparable to a single vessel model work.

人民解放軍海軍初の航空母艦

遼寧の前身はアドミラル・クズネツォフ級重航空巡洋艦2番艦ヴァリャーグである。ヴァリャーグは建造途中にソビエト連邦が崩壊し、未完成の船体はウクライナ海軍に編入。その後、中国海軍が購入し、001型航空母艦として建造が再開され、2012年9月に中華人民解放軍海軍待望の航空母艦として就役した。ロシア海軍が保有するアドミラル・クズネツォフと比べても、艦形自体に大きな変更は認められないが、VLSの撤去をはじめ、艤装類も中国海軍独自のものに置き換えられているため、その能力は別ものと考えられる。艦番号は16。なお、この「遼寧」を改良した中国海軍初の国産空母、002型航空母艦「山東」が2019年12月17日に就役している

The predecessor of the Liaoning was the second Admiral Kuznetsov-class heavy aircraft cruiser Varyag. The Soviet Union collapsed during the construction of the Varyag, and the incomplete hull was incorporated into the Ukrainian navy. Finally, the Chinese Navy purchased it, and construction was resumed as a Type 001 aircraft carrier. In September 2012, it was commissioned as a long-awaited aircraft carrier of People's Liberation Army Navy(PLAN). Compared to Admiral Kuznetsov, there is no significant change in the hull form itself, but the ship's equipment, including the removal of the VLS, has been replaced with equipment unique to the PLAN, and its capabilities are considered to be different. The ship number is 16. On December 17, 2019, the PLAN's first domestically produced aircraft carrier, Type 002 aircraft carrier "Shandong", was put into service as an improved version of the "Liaoning"

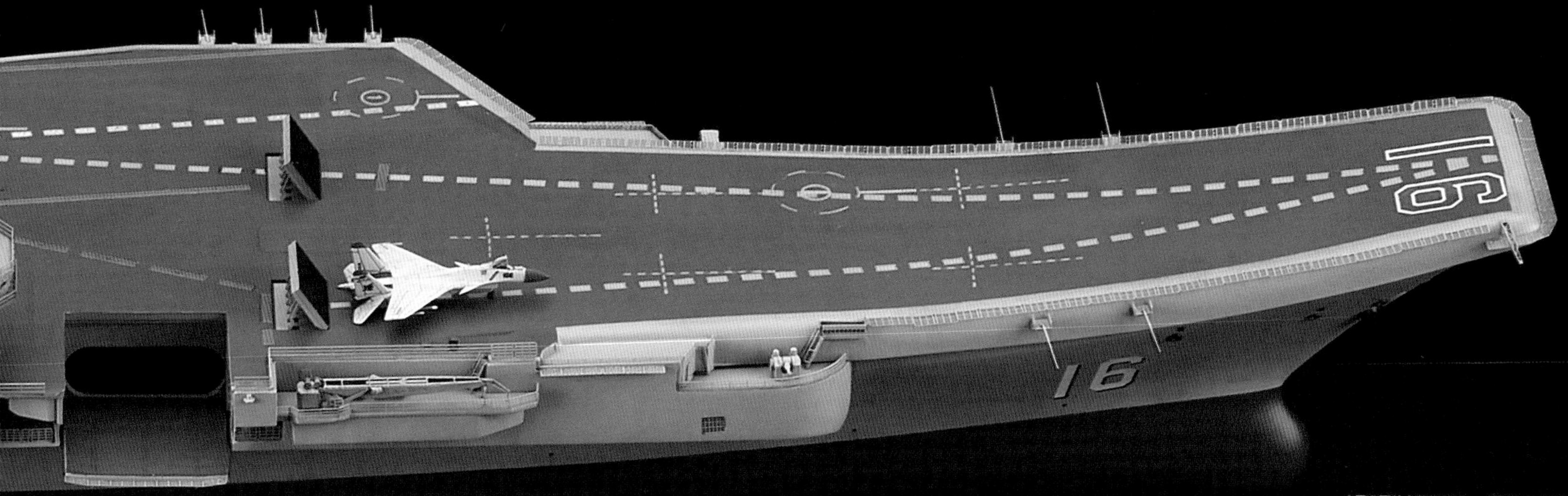

中国海軍航空母艦 遼寧
トランペッター 1／700 インジェクションプラスチックキット
TRUMPETER 1/700 PLA Navy Aircraft Carrier Liao Ning
Injection-plastic kit

遼寧は、2020年1月に開催される上海新年模型交流賽に笹原氏がゲストとして招かれたことがその製作の発端である。せっかく中国に招かれるのであれば、やはり現地のモデラーには中国艦船を見てもらったほうが喜ばれるのではないか、と考え製作を開始した。笹原氏はスケールアヴィエーション2019年3月号(Vol.126)において、トランペッター1/700 ロシア海軍航空母艦アドミラル・クズネツォフを製作している。実艦の生い立ちと同様、遼寧のキットはクズネツォフのバリエーションモデルで、アイランドと艤装関係以外は共通のパーツで構成される。クズネツォフで工作に難儀した個所は、その攻略法も含めてまだ記憶に新しい。ディテールアップ用の専用エッチングパーツも発売されており、製作はそんなに苦労しないであろうと考えていた。くわえて遼寧ではアイランドや格納庫内にLEDによる電飾のギミックを盛り込み、より見栄えのするプランを立案。結論からいえば、この選択こそが笹原氏を苦しめることになったのだが、本作はその甲斐あって素晴らしく精密に作り込まれたディテールと、今の模型トレンドである発光ギミックの搭載を両立させている。なお笹原氏が航空母艦を製作する際のスタンスは“艦載機のための見栄えの良い展示台”であり、本作でも中国海軍戦闘機J-15の搭載を予定している。作例では、19年12月にピットロードより発売された「1/700 世界の最新ステルス戦闘機セット2020」に含まれるのSu-35sのテストショットを入手、これをJ-15として製作している。■

The production of the Liaoning began when Mr. Sasahara was invited as a guest at the Shanghai New Year model festival held in January 2020. He thought that if they were to be invited to China, local modelers would be more pleased to see the Chinese ships, so he started building the carrier. In the March 2019 issue of Scale Aviation (Vol. 126), Sasahara produced the Trumpeter's 1/700 Russian Navy aircraft carrier Admiral Kuznetsov. Just like the real ship, the Liaoning kit is a variation of Kuznetsov and parts are common except for the island and rigging. Kuznetsov build had some difficult steps and those are still fresh in his memory. There's also a dedicated photo etched part for detailing, and he thought it wouldn't be too hard to build this time. In addition, he chooses to incorporate LED lighting gimmick into the island and hangar to make it look better. In short, it was this choice that made Sasahara suffer. But the result combines the brilliant, finely crafted details with the current model trend of lighting gimmick. Sasahara's main goal when he built the aircraft carrier is "build an attractive showcase for aircraft" and this time he plans to place the Chinese naval fighter J-15 on the deck. In this work, he obtained some test shot of Su-35s included in "1/700 World's Latest Stealth Fighter Set 2020" released from Pitroad in December 2019 and made them as J-15

遼寧は、基本的にはキットをストレートに組み、専用エッチングパーツや汎用エッチングパーツを用いて細部をディテールアップしている。また最新空母・山東用のエッチングパーツセットも購入したのだが、こちらについてはディテールに差があり過ぎて一部を使用するにとどまっている。また船体に施された補強板のディテールをマスキングテープとサーフェイサーの厚吹きで再現したり、艦載機格納庫のフロアを作成するといった工作は、クズネツォフと同様に行なっている

The Liaoning basically built straight out of the box, with both specific and general photo etched parts set to add detail. he also bought a set for the latest aircraft carrier Shandong, but the details are so different that he only uses some of them. Like Kuznetsov, it recreates the details of the reinforcing plates on the hull with masking tape and thick blowing of surfacer, and creates the floor of the aircraft hangar.

TRUMPETER 1/700 Scale
PLA Navy Aircraft Carrier Liao Ning

塗装はGSIクレオスのラッカー系塗料でキットの指定カラーに則って基本塗装を行ない、エナメル系塗料によるウォッシングと油彩による錆などの表現を施し、最終的にデカール保護のツヤ消しクリアーを全体に掛け完成となる。現用艦に限らず、笹原氏は過剰なウェザリングは行わない。ウォッシングもディテールの凹凸をハッキリさせることが目的で、例えば冬季迷彩の剥がれを再現するような特別な場合を除き、きれいな“生きている鑑”として仕上げるのが流儀なのだ

The basic paint is done with GSI Creos lacquer paint according to the designated color from the kit instruction. The washing by enamel paint and the rust effects are done with oil paint. Finally, flat clear for decal protection is applied over the whole hull and the deck. Sasahara does not apply excessive weathering. Washing is aimed at making the details stand out, and it is customary to finish it as a beautiful "a living ship" except in special cases such as reproduction of damaged winter camouflage.

アドミラル・クズネツォフと遼寧との差異については、やはりアイランド部分の形状が大きく印象が異なる。大型のアンテナやマストが林立するクズネツォフに対し、かなりすっきりとした印象の遼寧。ステルス性を考慮したと思しきそのスタイルこそが、最新の航空母艦であることを如実に物語っているのだ。また船体の塗装についても海上で目立ちにくいシンプルな洋上迷彩が施されており、その没個性的ないでたちこそが中国の最新航空母艦というキャラクターを語っている

Between Admiral Kuznetsov and Liaoning, the shape of the island is very different. Compared to Kuznetsov, which has large antennas and masts, the Liaoning has a clean and simple impression. The style that seems to take stealth into account clearly shows that it is the latest aircraft carrier. The painting of the ship's hull also features a simple marine camouflage that is inconspicuous on the sea, and its lack of individuality shows the character of China's latest aircraft carrier.

16

102

TRUMPETER 1/700 Scale PLA Navy Aircraft Carrier Liao Ning

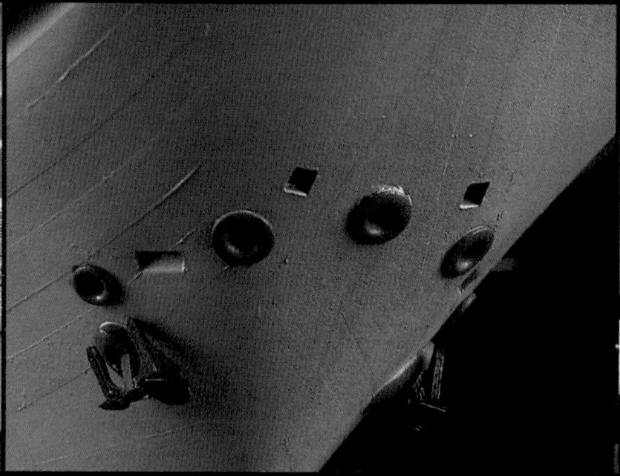

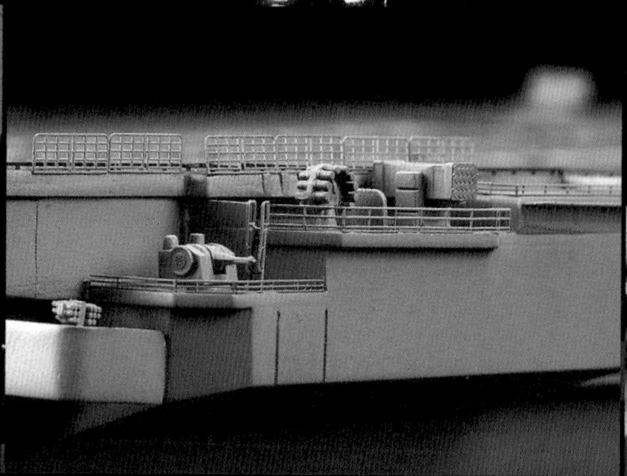

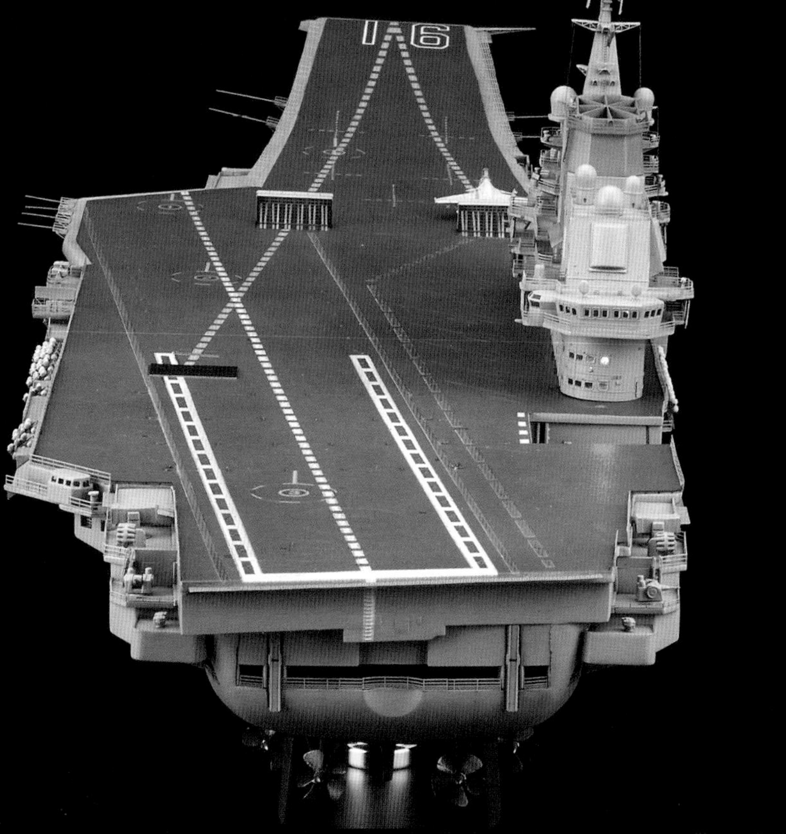

笹原氏のこれまでの作品と同様に、航空母艦はあくまで“作り込まれた1/700艦載機のための展示台”がテーマである。ニミッツではF-14やA-6、クズネツォフではSu-35といった艦載機の主翼を畳み、キャノピーをヒートプレスで自作して開放状態にし、エンジンノズルの金属ひき物パーツとして外注してきた。遼寧ではJ-15はピットロードのステルス戦闘機セットのものを使用､脚やパイロンはエッチングパーツセットに置き換えることでそのディテール情報量を引き上げている

As in Sasahara's previous works, the theme of aircraft carriers built is "an exhibition bench 1/700 aircraft." With Nimitz, F-14 and A -6, and with Kuznetsov, Su-35 were modified with folded wings and the canopy was made by heat press. , The J-15 on the Liaoning are from Pitroad's "stealth fighter sets." Landing gear and pylon are replaced with photo etched parts to increase the amount of detail information.

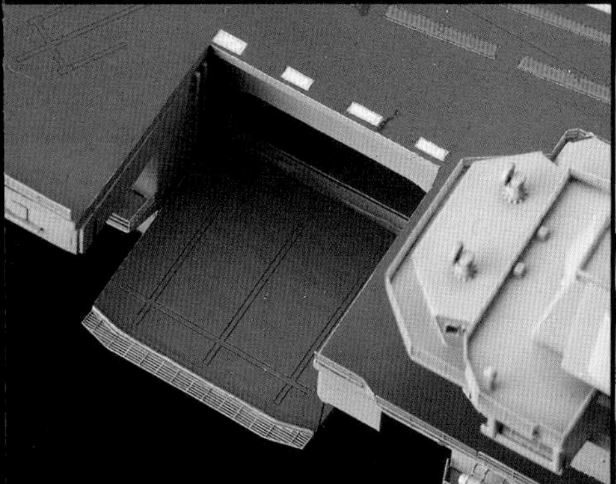

笹原 大　関連書籍

笹原 大の艦船模型 ナノ・テクノロジー工廠

1/700スケールという艦船模型の中であって世界最高峰の精密さを誇る笹原作品は実物を目の前にしてもその実像をけっして肉眼でとらえることはできない。そんな超精密作品をカメラで限界まで拡大して掲載。また笹原氏オリジナルの工具やハウツー記事なども満載、"ナノ・テクノロジー"と称される常識はずれの超精密工作の裏側を大公開

判型：A4判ソフトカバー
頁数：112ページ
発売中　定価（本体3800円+税）／大日本絵画刊

R工廠 超巧造艦ワークス 笹原 大 1/700 艦船模型集

1/700艦船模型のスペシャリスト、笹原 大が作り出した作品を集めた待望の1冊が遂に発刊!! 艦船模型専門誌『ネイビーヤード』、総合模型雑誌『月刊モデルグラフィックス』に掲載された、1/700 島風、1/700 秋津洲、1/700 青葉を中心に、本書用に新たに再撮影、製作過程の写真も掲載時より大幅に追加して再構成。また、作り起こし作品として1/700 第11昭南丸も掲載。笹原氏の超絶作品を製作手順を追って存分に味わうことのできる一冊となっている

判型：A4判ソフトカバー
頁数：64ページ
発売中　定価（本体3000円+税）／大日本絵画刊

関連雑誌

隔月刊スケールアヴィエーション

模型ジャンルのなかでもっとも伝統ある飛行機模型の楽しみ方を、あらゆる角度から探るエアクラフトモデラーの専門誌

偶数月13日発売
定価（本体1344円+税）／大日本絵画刊

2020年1月号 特別定価（本体2500円＋税）

ネイビーヤード

戦車模型専門誌『月刊アーマーモデリング』の姉妹誌。大戦艦から現用艦まで、幅広いテーマで艦船模型専門誌

年3回刊行　3・7・11月の5日迄に発売
定価（本体2286円+税）／大日本絵画刊

HOW TO BUILD 1/700 SCALE
MODERN AIRCRAFT CAREER
HANDBOOK
HOW TO BUILD 1/700 現用航空母艦ハンドブック

著　笹原 大

編集　スケールアヴィエーション編集部

協力　寒河江雅樹

発行日　2020年1月20日　初版第1刷

発行人　小川光二

発行所　株式会社 大日本絵画
〒101-0054 東京都千代田区神田錦町1丁目7番地
Tel. 03-3294-7861（代表）
URL. http://www.kaiga.co.jp

企画・編集　株式会社 アートボックス
〒101-0054 東京都千代田区神田錦町1丁目7番地
錦町一丁目ビル4F
Tel. 03-6820-7000（代表）　Fax. 03-5281-8467
URL. http://www.modelkasten.com/

◎内容に関するお問い合わせ先：03(6820)7000　㈱アートボックス
◎販売に関するお問い合わせ先：03(3294)7861　㈱大日本絵画

Publisher: Dainippon Kaiga Co., Ltd.
Kanda Nishiki-cho 1-7, Chiyoda-ku, Tokyo 101-0054 Japan
Phone 81-3-3294-7861
Dainippon Kaiga URL. http://www.kaiga.co.jp.

Editor: ARTBOX Co.,Ltd.
Nishikicho 1-chome bldg., 4th Floor, Kanda Nishiki-cho 1-7, Chiyoda-ku, Tokyo
101-0054 Japan
Phone 81-3-6820-7000
ARTBOX URL: http://www.modelkasten.com/

ISBN 978-4-499-00107-6

＊本書は『隔月刊スケールアヴィエーション』2017年1月号（Vol.113）および、2019年03月号（126号）、『ネイビーヤード VOL.41』に掲載した作品をもとに、新たな作品を加えたものです